O9-AII-131

IN PRAISE OF
PECANS

IN PRAISE OF PECANS

RECIPES & RECOLLECTIONS

JUNE JACKSON

PHOTOGRAPHY BY WATT M. CASEY, JR.

BRIGHT SKY PRESS

BRIGHT SKY PRESS

Box 416
Albany, Texas 76430

Text copyright © 2007 by June L. Jackson
Photographs copyright © 2007 by Watt M. Casey, Jr.

No part of this book may be reproduced in any form or by any
electronic or mechanical means, including information storage and
retrieval devices or systems, without prior written permission from
the publisher, except that brief passages may be quoted for reviews.

10   9   8   7   6   5   4   3   2   1

Library of Congress Cataloging-in-Publication Data

Jackson, June.
    In praise of pecans : recipes and recollections / by June Jackson.
        p. cm.
    Includes bibliographical references and index.
    ISBN 978-1-933979-00-7 (jacketed hardcover : alk. paper) 1.
Cookery (Pecans) I. Title.

    TX814.2.P4J32 2007
    641.6'452—dc22   2007008725

Book and cover design by Isabel Lasater Hernandez
Edited by Kristine Krueger

Printed in China through Asia Pacific Offset

This book is lovingly dedicated to my mother,
Kathryn Heimbach Lang Reynolds
January 20, 1916–February 22, 2001

TABLE OF CONTENTS

PREFACE

It was a sunny fall Saturday in Bethesda, Maryland, and somewhere in the country, pecans were being harvested, but not there. Maryland is too far north for growing pecans.

As a Southerner transplanted to the North, I remembered the thrill of the fall pecan harvest back home. Each September, I became nostalgic, imagining I could smell the acrid scent of the trees' leaves. I longed to see the grape-like clusters of nuts on the branches sporting the sharp green color of their husks before falling to the ground.

Although I ordered the nuts from my hometown growers in Louisiana and kept them refrigerated year-round, I still felt distanced from the indigenous assumptions one can make when living in proximity to pecan groves. My longing reminded me of an English friend who had relocated to the United States. Once when I asked her what she missed most about home, she answered immediately, "The primroses in the spring!"

My answer would have been, "Seeing pecans growing on the trees ... and hearing them fall to the ground!" Falling acorns make a nice sound as well, but the "ping" and "thud" don't herald the consumption of a delicious, nutritious treat—unless you happen to be a squirrel.

Cooking with pecans took some of the sting out of being away from them geographically. The roasted ones, the ones in pies, cakes, cookies and cereals—all of them reminded me of home. The more I missed pecans, the more I shoved them onto other people in hopes that they would get the message of the nuts' usefulness.

Once when I was planning a fall luncheon, I was suffering from a bout of nostalgia, which explains the menu: I included pecans in every course—from roasted appetizers, through several pecan-laced salads and right up to the pecan-encrusted chicken breasts, followed by pecan-studded meringue baskets filled with mango sorbet.

Having cooked obsessively the previous day, I began to wonder a few hours before the guests arrived if I had gone too far in making my point. Then, after I'd served dessert, one of the guests asked, "You've really got a 'thing' for pecans, don't you?"

Since she was the person who had eaten the most—actually cleaned each plate—I took it to be a compliment of sorts.

A few days later, I had a call from one of my

luncheon guests, Colleen Nunn. She said her husband, Sam, wanted to meet with me about something. He was still in the Senate at the time, and I had no idea what he wanted. We agreed to meet the following Saturday.

As I entered their home, I found Sam reading a serious-looking book. Putting it down, he got right to the point: "June, as I travel around the country and the world, I'm shocked that pecans are so underused. Frankly, I love pecans—eat some every day—sometimes twice a day."

Liking pecans was second nature to Sam, the son of a Georgia pecan grower. He grew up around relatives who, in one way or another, were involved in the pecan industry. The dinner conversations of his youth frequently revolved around pecan use and promotion. With his personal penchant for pecans, he became puzzled at the worldwide use of walnuts, almonds, pistachios and even macadamia nuts, when the "Native American Nut" remained almost unheard of.

"I just don't understand it," he told me. "It really bothers me," he emphasized, sitting up straighter in his chair.

Nodding in agreement, I continued to wonder why he'd wanted to meet with me.

"Colleen told me you prepared a delicious luncheon recently and used pecans in every way imaginable," he stated.

"Yes, I did cook a few dishes!" I answered, slightly embarrassed.

Then he asked, "Do you think you could write a book that would promote pecan use around the world?" Never one to think small, he had already gone global in the name of pecans!

Affected by his enthusiasm, I didn't hesitate. "Sure," I answered, not knowing where I would start. Once I agreed, the meeting appeared to be over. Thankfully, he didn't press me for details. He liked short meetings, and I had no more to say without time to think over his idea.

Confident with the mandate, I left the Nunns' home determined to answer the call. Although some time has passed since that fall day, I've kept my promise.

Sam ignited my desire to write about pecans, but meanwhile, I had lived with them as a backdrop for social and family life since childhood.

Pecans are to me what dates are to Moroccans, pine nuts are to Middle Easterners and almonds are to Californians. A friend who'd grown up in California's almond country once told me that when he went home for Christmas during his college years, he waited for one sensory impression to tell him that the holidays had begun. "I would open the door and know it was Christmas because I could smell the almonds roasting in the oven. My mom always had them waiting for me."

When I was a child, and old enough to dread summer's end and the resumption of school, I placated myself by remembering that fall brought with it the pecan harvest—a fresh crop of my favorite nuts!

Dissatisfied with living in what I saw as a "bland" area of the country, I searched for one indigenous, edible reason why my southern Louisiana hometown was notable. Of course, at that time, the town was surrounded by some of the South's most fertile cotton fields, but I wanted an edible notability!

Thinking of the citrus groves of Florida, and the avocado crops of California, I envied those areas' ability to produce something of a special, gourmet nature.

It was not until I lodged this complaint with my mother that I was relieved of that burden of envy. "What are you talking about?" she questioned. "Don't you realize that we grow premium-quality pecans all around Winnsboro? Our paper shells are hard to beat!"

Immediately curious about the definition of "paper shells" (a thinner-shelled variety of pecan), I was pacified for the moment. Leaving the kitchen, I went outside and heard some pecans fall from my neighbor's tree and felt glad.

I'll never know whether my mother said what she did just to stop my childish rantings about

wanting to live elsewhere, like the San Fernando Valley, or if her pride of place was sincere. Nevertheless, I fell in love with pecans at the age of 7 and have never let go.

In time, I developed an affection for pecans for many other reasons—their taste, texture, adaptability—more reliably mature reasons for devotion; the initial passion, however, was born out of a child's need for civic pride.

I was grateful to pecans then, as now. They have been good to me.

—June Jackson
St. Simons Island, Georgia
Fall 2006

11

MY LIFETIME WITH PECANS

Years after a 25-year-old Thomas Edison invented waxed paper in 1872, my mother began making pecan-filled candies and scooping them onto large pieces of the nonstick waxed surface. As a girl of 12—that would have been in 1928—she cut a praline recipe out of the Monroe, Louisiana, newspaper; and she never wavered from its dictates.

As far as I know, she made her last batch of pralines in February 2001, a few days before she died. She used that same recipe, the one people had begged off her for over 60 years, and its goodness never failed her.

When my mother got out the waxed paper, I knew she was getting ready to make candy. I had seen her reach for the skinny box, colored the same light blue and red, for as long as I could remember. This gesture meant she had an urge to make candy, be it divinity, date loaf, caramel fudge or pralines.

Sometimes the urge would seize her for no particular reason. Walking home from work at the Princess Theater, she might get a taste for caramel fudge. On such occasions, she would enter the house, kick off her shoes, go to the kitchen and take out the waxed paper, thus setting the stage for the sweet morsels that were to come. Other times, I could persuade her to make the candy I was hungry for. Without fail, her response would be, "If you help me pick out the pecans, I'll make the candy."

As I remember, large sacks of unshelled pecans were commonplace in most homes in the South. I don't know where we got them, but there they sat in the closet, waiting to be used when needed. We never had pecan trees in our yard, so someone must have given them to us. Grocery stores didn't sell pecans, other than the "Funstens" brand in a tin, and those just wouldn't do for candymaking, according to my mother.

Picking out pecans was the scourge of my early youth. Even though most candy recipes called for only one cup of the wondrous pieces ("Not a scant cup, either," Mother would remind), the job of loosening the nutmeat seemed endless to a child. After the adults had used the nutpicks, we had the job of extracting

13

the little pieces because our hands were small enough to reach into the tiny crevices.

"Don't leave anything behind in the shell," we were instructed. "Pecans are too expensive to waste any." Of course, we were given all the pecans we ever used, but somewhere, pecans must have been costly.

Had my mother's candy not been so good, the onerous job of furnishing the picked-out nuts wouldn't have been worth the trouble. With some varieties, Mother could start the candy cooking and sit down at the kitchen table to help me pick out the pecans. In a race against the clock, we could have the required amount just at the end, when she needed to add them to the thickening, boiling ingredients. Pralines, though, were a different matter. Mother would demand that we have the tall glass already filled so when the perfect moment came, she would have what she needed.

The "tall glass" was a regular water glass, not a measuring cup. "When it's full, that's

My mother, Kathryn H. Lang Reynolds, age 25, 1941, Winnsboro, La.

14

the right amount of pecans for pralines," Mother always said. When I saw that glass on the counter, it was a sure sign pralines were to be made and pecans were to be picked out.

As I got older and had friends come to the house, we divided up the pecan task: One girl would crack the nuts with a hammer while two others took pointed picks and loosened the meat—in pieces—to drop into the cup or glass. To get a whole pecan half to come out of the shell in one piece was considered quite a feat. I was grown before I saw many pecan halves; by then, machines did the work for us.

When we girls presented the readied nuts to my mother, she would ask, "Did you get all the pieces of pulp out of them? If you didn't, they will make my candy bitter." She told me later that someone in the group was not a careful "picker," and she mentioned the girl by name. "You've got to watch her," my mother warned, as if my friend were as venal as any thief.

At long last, when the candy was ready to be ladled up in sinful, sugary pieces onto the waxed paper, we girls would drool just looking at the marvelous sight.

"Mrs. Lang, how long till we can eat the candy?" one of the group would inevitably inquire, hungrily eyeing the counter filled with our perfectly wrought afternoon treat.

"Oh, not long now; it just has to harden a few

more minutes," my mother would answer.

The wait seemed interminable to starving girls who felt they had earned the right to dive into the divinity, caramel fudge or pralines by suffering the painful process of nut picking.

Of all the joys of those times in the kitchen with my mother at the candy pot—the scents, the sight and the taste ... not to mention the comfort—what I cherish to this day is the fact that once we paid the price by tediously picking out the pecans, the candy was not rationed. My mother never told us, "Now you can have one piece each." Abundance reigned!

We were free to eat until we were full. No one counted out the portion size; we just sat there eating candy until some other activity caught our fancy. Having washed up her candy pot and put it away, Mother would go into the living room to do the crossword puzzle in the evening paper, saying on her way out of the kitchen, "Have fun, girls."

Candy did mean fun, despite the work involved ... at least when we were at home. On the road, it was another story. When we left on car trips, my even-tempered mother would turn snippy. Cooped up going to see my father's relatives, she would withdraw into herself. To make matters worse, it wasn't long before Dad would want to stop at a Stuckey's candy store for a cup of coffee and "something sweet."

I was 4 years old in '41, wearing my beloved white boots and acting up in front of the camera due to jealousy at my mother's holding my 2-month-old cousin, "Little Jimmy" Baur.

15

There always seemed to be a Stuckey's, wherever our destination, since these shops dotted the countryside at that time. The cash register was wisely placed so that Mrs. Stuckey's candies faced the traveler upon leaving the store.

Usually, my dad resisted the temptation to buy candy, as he knew how jealous my mother was of Mrs. Stuckey's success; however, the pecan logs turned his head. He never went on a car trip without buying a pecan log. I think it had something to do with the fact that Mother didn't make pecan logs ... thus, he was not openly turning traitor.

All dressed up for my fourth-grade piano recital in spring 1947, Winnsboro, La.

16

Back in the car, Dad would say diplomatically, "All right—now who wants a bite of this pecan log?"

Sulking in front, my mother would look at the candy and say, "No, thank you." Feeling disloyal but overpowered by my sweet tooth, I would grab a piece and retreat to the backseat to devour it.

As we drove away, I waited for my mother's comment, which always came. "My candy puts hers to shame," she would announce to the windshield. "If I opened a candy shop, I could put Mrs. Stuckey out of business."

After riding along abstemiously for a few miles, Mother would pick up the paper bag that contained the offending candy and say, "Well, I'll have just one bite." Then, savoring the sweetness, she would unfailingly add, "This is good, but Mrs. Stuckey better never try her hand at pralines!"

From the backseat, I felt relieved that we had followed my mother into the pit of envy one more time and come back out with the help of confidence-building pralines. I knew the rest of the trip could now turn enjoyable.

More than 50 years after my family squirmed through those trips, in a wondrous twist of fate, I became friends with the next generation of Stuckeys—in Washington, D.C.

When one of our children got married, various friends of the bride/groom would get together to give a luncheon for out-of-town guests. Since the guest list was usually sizable, we'd often have the party at the Stuckeys' home, as it was roomy and inviting.

I was responsible for bringing dessert to one such luncheon, so I asked my mother to make several batches of pralines. Always happy to get out her tall glass and praline pot, she agreed to furnish "all the pralines that crowd can eat." She liked the idea of a lot of people devouring her specialty.

The day of the party, I staggered up the Stuckeys' walk, carrying a huge silver tray laden with over 100 freshly made, perfect pralines. Getting them safely

My mother holding her dog, "Muffin," at Thanksgiving 2000, St. Simons Island, Ga.

to the stately sideboard in the dining room, I breathed more easily. As if on cue, the present-day Mrs. Stuckey, the late entrepreneur's daughter-in-law, reached for one praline, ate it and then took another.

She walked away, only to return shortly for a third "sample." Her eyes large and excited, she called out, "June, this is the best candy I've ever eaten in my entire life! How can I get more?" With this, she reached for a fourth praline.

When no one was looking, I went to the phone to tell my mother she had been vindicated. First, she gloated. Then she told me, "I never thought I'd live to hear that!"

During my last visit with Mother in 2001, I watched her as she carefully cut the waxed paper and laid it out on the counter. Getting out not The Glass, but one of the exact same size, she tacitly indicated she was going to make pralines. How familiar these gestures!

Eighty-five then and still beautiful, my mother lovingly dished up the last piece of rich, caramel-colored candy, predictably the 22nd one of the batch. Modest about most of her achievements, my mother bragged about her pralines. I waited for her to say, "You know, these are good enough to serve to anybody!" And she did, as she proudly took the first bite.

Sitting down at the kitchen table, she said to me, "I've decided how long I want to live."

My family loves my food and encourages my writing. Here we are in early 2006 in Los Angeles: my sons, Hayes (left) and Scott; Hayes's wife, Cooper, and their boys, Whit (left), Graeme (with me) and Davis, plus Scott's dog, "Lucy."

Blanching at the thought of her not being around, I asked, "You do?"

With a knowing look, she added, "Yes, I want to live as long as I can make perfect pralines."

By that reckoning, it was not time for her to leave. But 10 days later, she was gone.

Good Cooking and Fine Eating with Pecans

Other than its delectable flavor, an important trait of the pecan is its adaptability. From the first course, through the entrée and the salad course, this nut can add much to the enjoyment of any meal. Don't forget dessert—saving what some diners think is the best part of any eating experience until the meal's end, pecans are omnipresent in pies, cakes, cookies, candies and puddings. What holiday dinner would be complete without pecan pie?

As a snack food, pecans rate very high in nutrition, flavor and convenience: They are at their most nutritious in the raw state, simply eaten out of hand. Paired with dried fruits in trail mix, they provide the outdoorsman with sustenance while hiking, biking or fishing. Few other "take-alongs" measure up to the food value of pecans. High-quality "portable food" is difficult to come by, and pecans can be stored and kept ready for the most sudden departure from home.

Whether enjoying them while walking under a nut-laden tree in the fall ... waiting for a cluster to fall to the ground ... or dining royally on pecan-encrusted mountain trout in an elegant restaurant, the discriminating consumer begins to understand how good this product of nature is, in all its incarnations.

Useful in halves, pieces or ground into a tasty meal for baking, pecans have enhanced our lives for centuries. However, in today's kitchens and laboratories, they are finally being recognized for their versatility and nutritive value.

Even doctors are recommending pecans as a valuable source of protein in snacking and as an addition to every aspect of our diets. But they remind the patient that the caloric content of pecans is high, thus they counsel moderation in consumption. Portion size is the key to healthy eating, and the right amount of pecans, consumed regularly, can aid in nutrition.

So here's to your healthy, pecan-filled eating pleasure!

STARTERS
Snacks, Nibbles and Treats

Pecans are a snack you can enjoy right off the tree! If you should be fortunate enough to find yourself in a pecan orchard in the fall, just bend over, pick the nut up off the ground, crack it, pick the meat out and eat it on the spot. Nature prepares the pecan so that no cooking is necessary—from tree to ground to mouth in a matter of seconds.

Once the industrial methods of harvesting, cracking and shelling have taken place, you can order pecans from a myriad of sources (for a listing, see pages 170–173). When possible, buy the current year's crop.

The easiest way to enjoy pecans is to reach into the airtight tin you've stored the nuts in and eat a few pieces. If you have them in the freezer, it takes almost no time to wait for them to thaw. Pecans can be frozen for up to 2 years without losing flavor or nutritive value.

It's almost as easy to mix raw pecans with a few ingredients and turn them into an appetizing treat. Whether toasted, roasted, or added to a snack mix or spread, the variety is endless.

Hot-Sweet Party Pecans

A variety of flavors meet in this recipe—salty, sweet, spicy and just good. These pecans are great to have on hand, and they can stay in the freezer for times when you need something fast ... either when company is coming or when you feel a sudden hunger for something satisfying.

2 to 4 tablespoons butter
¼ cup whiskey or bourbon
2 tablespoons sugar
2 tablespoons hot pepper sauce*
1½ teaspoons salt
½ teaspoon garlic powder
4 cups pecan halves

Preheat oven to 310°. In a saucepan, combine the first six ingredients. Bring to a boil and boil for 3 minutes, stirring to blend flavors. Add pecans and toss to coat well.

Spread in a single layer on a baking sheet. Bake for 15 minutes; stir. Bake 15 minutes longer. Cool; store in an airtight container. After 2 weeks, store in the freezer.

Yield: 4 cups

*Using chipotle pepper sauce will add a smoky flavor.

21

Toasting and Roasting Pecans

Heating raw pecans for about 5–7 minutes in a 325° oven will bring out the nutty flavor even more. Another toasting method is to heat them in a skillet on top of the stove, shaking the nuts so they don't burn. A low temperature is adequate, and no salt is necessary.

Slightly spicier than simple toasted pecans, but just as good for snacking or using as starters, roasted pecans can be prepared in a variety of ways.

Whether savory, sweet or spicy, each recipe has merit, depending on its use. See Hot-Sweet Party Pecans above, Simple Roasted Pecans on page 22, Smoky Roasted Pecans and Savory Nuts on page 23 and Sweet Spiced Nuts on page 28.

Simple Roasted Pecans

Different from toasted pecans, this method adds other flavors and can be served with cocktails.

1 to 2 tablespoons butter, melted
2 teaspoons finely ground sea salt or table salt
1 teaspoon Worcestershire sauce
2 cups pecans (preferably halves)

Preheat oven to 310°.* In a bowl, combine the butter, salt and Worcestershire sauce. Add pecans and toss to coat well. Spread in a single layer on a baking sheet. Bake for 10 minutes; stir. Bake 10–15 minutes longer or until golden brown. Do not allow them to burn, as the nuts will acquire a bitter taste.

Yield: 2 cups

*Some recipes recommend an oven temperature of 350° and a shorter baking time. The slower, lower-temperature method produces a "riper" flavor.

Smoky Roasted Pecans

Again proving pecans' adaptability, this recipe adds another flavor with which the nut can be enjoyed. If you like "heat," use the pepper sauce.

2 cups pecans (preferably halves)
1 to 3 teaspoons liquid smoke or chipotle
   pepper sauce
1 to 2 tablespoons butter, melted
1 teaspoon salt

Preheat oven to 310°. In a bowl, coat pecans with liquid smoke or pepper sauce; let stand for 15 minutes. Combine the butter and salt; pour over pecans and toss to coat well. Spread in a single layer on a baking sheet. Bake for 10 minutes; stir. Bake 10–15 minutes longer or until golden brown.

Yield: 2 cups

Savory Nuts

This recipe provides still another non-sweet method for enjoying pecans, which pair very well with herbs as well as spices.

2 tablespoons white wine Worcestershire sauce
1 tablespoon pecan oil* or olive oil
½ teaspoon dried thyme, crushed
¼ teaspoon dried rosemary, crushed
¼ teaspoon black pepper or ⅛ teaspoon ground
   red pepper
2 cups pecan halves (pieces can be used in salads)

Preheat oven to 350°. In a bowl, combine the Worcestershire sauce, oil, thyme, rosemary and pepper. Add pecans and coat well. Spread in a single layer on a baking sheet. Bake for 6 minutes; stir. Bake 6–9 minutes longer or until golden brown. Cool; store in an airtight container.

Yield: 2 cups

*Pecan oil is now being marketed by several companies. Lighter than olive oil, it is a healthy addition to salad dressings and good for pan-searing meats and general cooking use. To find out where it's available, see the Source Guide on page 170.

23

Peace Pecans

These pecans got their name when they were served at a dinner party in Washington, D.C. By the time the hostess served the first course, a serious political argument had broken out. Seemingly nothing could dissuade the guests from clinging to their opposing views.

The entrée was delicious but barely noticed by the diners. A beautiful dessert came and went with no comment other than those made by the warring parties. Finally, in desperation, the host turned to his wife and said, "Maybe you'd better get out those white pecans." Then he whispered, "I don't think they're ever going home!"

Far into the night, these pecans were passed around the table, then three of the guests asked, "What ARE these? They're delicious!" Two people from the other side of the argument answered, "I agree!"

Relieved, the hostess added, "At last, we've agreed on something; from now on, I'm going to call these my 'Peace Pecans'!"

24

2 tablespoons butter, melted
1½ teaspoons finely ground sea salt or table salt
2 cups pecan halves
1 package (10 to 12 ounces) vanilla or white chips

Preheat oven to 325°. In a bowl, combine butter and salt. Add pecans and toss to coat well. Spread in a single layer on a baking sheet. Bake for 10 minutes; stir. Bake 15–20 minutes longer.

Meanwhile, in a heavy skillet over very low heat, melt the chips, stirring constantly. (Patience is necessary; if heated too fast, the chips will "blister" and become unusable.) When fully melted to the consistency of cake icing, remove from the heat and add the roasted pecans gradually, stirring gently to coat.

When thoroughly coated, spread on waxed paper. "Rake" nuts with a spoon to separate into individual pieces or small clusters. Cool; break into desired size pieces. Store in a plastic bag or airtight container.

Yield: about 3 cups

GOCP–Good Old Cherries and Pecans

"GOCP" is a variation of "GORP"—a trail mix, which is known in the United Kingdom, New Zealand, Australia and Iraq as "scroggin."

While the Oxford English Dictionary of 1913 used "gorp" as a verb meaning "to eat greedily," hikers, bikers and other outdoorsmen think of GORP as meaning "Good Old Raisins and Peanuts" or, for our purpose, "Good Old Cherries and Pecans."

Some recreation buffs buy their trail mix; others prefer to make their own. Various combinations of high-energy, nutritious foods suffice on a hike, as long as they are nonperishable, lightweight and biodegradable. Leave no trash on the trail!

Common ingredients in GORP are numerous and allow for personal preference. Nuts, seeds, dried fruits and cereals, yogurt chips, chocolate chunks or M&M's can be combined in any proportion, depending on taste and appetite. Try dried unsweetened coconut flakes, if you can find them at a health food store. GOCP makes a colorful holiday "nibble" when served in a candy dish.

1 cup dried cherries
1 cup pecan halves or pieces
1 cup flaked coconut
½ cup roasted salted pepitas (pumpkin seeds)
½ cup chocolate pieces or chunks, optional

In a bowl, combine all ingredients and mix well. Divide into 1-cup portions in plastic bags, if traveling immediately. For snacking at home, store in a 1-quart plastic bag, airtight jar or tin for 2 weeks.

Without the chocolate pieces, GOCP can be added to oatmeal cookie dough or a sweet bread such as banana or pumpkin. For mixing in a baked recipe, add about ½ cup of GOCP to the batter. For use as a topping for sweet breads, sprinkle about ¼ cup GOCP over the batter before baking.

Yield: 3½-4 cups

27

A "Divot" of Pecans

A portion size of pecans is considered a "divot"—the amount of nuts that fits into the palm of one's hand: about eight halves for a small hand or 14 for a big hand. For a simple snack with "staying power," enjoy a divot of pecans with a few slices of apple.

Sweet Spiced Nuts

Sweetened pecans are good tossed in salads just before serving. These make a delicious snack and are also nice to package for gift-giving.

1 egg white
1 teaspoon water
4 cups pecan halves (pieces can be used in salads)
1 cup sugar or ½ cup maple or cane syrup
1 teaspoon ground cinnamon
½ teaspoon salt, optional
¼ teaspoon freshly grated nutmeg
¼ teaspoon ground allspice

Preheat oven to 325°. In a large bowl, whisk egg white and water (also add syrup at this point if using it instead of sugar). Add pecans and toss to coat. Combine the sugar (unless you are using syrup), cinnamon, salt if desired, nutmeg and allspice; sprinkle over nuts and toss to coat well. Spread in a single layer on a greased baking sheet. Bake for 10 minutes; stir. Bake 10 minutes longer. Spread on waxed paper to cool. Store in an airtight container.

Yield: 4 cups

Candied Gingered Pecans

Although this recipe pairs pecans with still another spice, it is clear that the two flavors are very compatible. These gingered nuts fit nicely in a trail mix or candy dish ... or add them to a salad such as the Wintertime Relief Salad (recipe on page 41).

½ cup coarsely chopped pecans
3 tablespoons sugar
¼ teaspoon ground ginger

Line a small baking sheet with foil and grease the foil with butter; set aside. In a small skillet, combine all ingredients. Cook over medium-low heat, shaking, not stirring, occasionally. When sugar melts, reduce heat to low. Continue cooking until sugar is golden brown, stirring enough to keep mixture from burning or sticking to the pan. Pour onto prepared baking sheet; cool. Break into small pieces.

Yield: about ½ cup

Crispy Cocktail Wafers

These crunchy wafers have been popular for years and are a favorite with nibblers of all ages. Sometimes I'll place a pecan half on each wafer before baking.

1 cup butter, softened
2 cups (8 ounces) shredded sharp or extra sharp
   Cheddar cheese
2 cups all-purpose flour
2 cups Rice Krispies
⅓ cup ground pecans
⅛ teaspoon cayenne pepper

Preheat oven to 375°. In a mixing bowl, cream the butter and cheese. Add flour, about ⅔ cup at a time, blending after each addition. Add cereal, pecans and cayenne; gently mix until well blended.

Shape into small balls or drop by small spoonfuls onto greased baking sheets; flatten with a fork to form round wafers. Bake for 10 minutes or until lightly browned. Cool; store in an airtight container.

Yield: about 4 dozen

29

Pecan-Laced Cheese Straws

Long a favorite in the South, these piquant treats go with a salad or a drink ... just by themselves, they make a great snack.

⅔ cup butter, softened
2 cups (8 ounces) shredded sharp or extra sharp
   Cheddar cheese
¼ cup ground pecans
2 cups all-purpose flour
¼ teaspoon salt
⅛ teaspoon cayenne pepper

Preheat oven to 350°. In a mixing bowl, cream the butter, cheese and pecans. Add flour, salt and cayenne. Mix until fully workable, more so than pie dough.

Using a cookie press with the small star attachment, pipe dough into 4-inch-long strips onto ungreased baking sheets. Or roll out dough on a floured surface to desired thickness and cut into strips, then transfer to the baking sheets. Twist each strip once or twice. Bake for 10–15 minutes or until golden brown. Cool; store in an airtight container.

Yield: about 4 dozen

Cheddar Cornflake Wafers

Another accompaniment to cocktail time, these wafers also attain their crunch from the addition of pecans plus a venerable breakfast item.

½ cup butter, softened
2 cups (8 ounces) shredded sharp or extra sharp
   Cheddar cheese
¼ cup pecan pieces or ground pecans
1 cup all-purpose flour
¼ teaspoon salt
¼ teaspoon paprika
¼ teaspoon hot pepper sauce
1½ cups cornflakes

Preheat oven to 350°. In a mixing bowl, cream the butter and cheese. Add pecans, flour, salt, paprika and pepper sauce; mix well. After mixture is workable, add cornflakes, stirring lightly with a fork so as not to crush the cereal.

Pinch off pieces of dough and roll into marble-size pieces. Place on ungreased baking sheets; press down lightly, but not with enough pressure to crush the cereal. Bake for 10–12 minutes or until golden brown and flattened. Cool; store in an airtight container.

Yield: about 4 dozen

Blue Velvet Spread

Pecans go well with almost any cheese, especially blue, Cheddar, Brie and chèvre. Whether in, on or around these varieties of cheeses, pecans contribute to the flavor of a dish. Even with Gorgonzola, the strong Italian blue, the nutty flavor of pecans stands out.

Serve this spread with bland crackers as an appetizer or on its own as part of an after-dinner cheese plate. It also goes particularly well with a spinach salad and toast points.

12 ounces blue cheese, crumbled
1 package (8 ounces) cream cheese, softened
1 tablespoon dried or minced fresh chives
Splash of vermouth or whiskey, optional
¾ cup pecan pieces, toasted if desired

In a bowl, combine the cheeses, chives and vermouth or whiskey if desired. Form into a ball, loaf or desired shape; roll in pecans until coated. Serve at room temperature; chill to store.

Yield: 2 cups

Red Lentil Pecan Pâté

With toasted pita chips or baked tortilla chips, this spread makes a nutritious appetizer for a large group. Pecans also pair well with garbanzos and black beans, so try other combinations of legumes and seasonings to offer a hummus sampler.

2 cups dried red lentils, rinsed and sorted
1½ cups diced onions, *divided*
½ cup diced celery
4 cups vegetable broth
1 teaspoon soy sauce, optional
Salt and pepper to taste
1 tablespoon pecan oil *or* olive oil
2 to 3 cloves garlic, minced
1 tablespoon minced fresh basil *or* 1 teaspoon
   dried basil
1½ cups pecan pieces, lightly toasted
½ cup minced fresh parsley

In a large saucepan, combine the lentils, ¾ cup onions, celery and broth. Cook, uncovered, over medium heat for 10 minutes. Reduce heat; cover and simmer for 20 minutes or until lentils are tender and creamy. Remove from the heat. Add soy sauce if desired or season with salt and pepper; cool.

In a skillet, heat oil; sauté the garlic, basil and remaining onions until onions are translucent; cool. Transfer to a food processor; add the lentil mixture. Purée until smooth. Refrigerate any leftovers.

Yield: about 3 cups

Variation: For added flavor, mix 1 teaspoon pecan oil or olive oil with 1 teaspoon balsamic vinegar and "float" on top of pâté when serving.

Pecan-Studded Pinecone

This is a good recipe to make with children. They'll enjoy decorating the pinecone with the nuts, especially since many of them will have made peanut butter-pinecone bird feeders (only to have the squirrels get there first!). It's a perfect appetizer for a holiday party or buffet.

2 cups (8 ounces) shredded sharp *or* extra sharp Cheddar cheese

1 package (8 ounces) cream cheese, softened

2 tablespoons Major Gray chutney, optional

1 tablespoon dried *or* minced fresh chives

½ teaspoon cayenne pepper *or* chipotle pepper sauce

1 to 1¼ cups pecan halves, toasted if desired

In a mixing bowl, combine the cheeses. Add chutney if desired, chives and cayenne; mix well. Form into an elongated ball in the shape of an oversized pinecone. Insert the pecan halves into the cheese ball in a semi-vertical position to resemble a pinecone. Serve at room temperature with crackers; chill to store. Leftover cheese spread can be reshaped and redecorated.

Yield: about 2 cups

Ideas for Making Low-Carb Foods More Attractive

- Sprinkle chopped pecans over breakfast yogurt.
- When making deviled eggs, add some finely chopped pecans to the mixture or sprinkle over the top.
- Add chopped pecans to cooked green beans; think of it as providing extra nutrition as well as crunch!
- Stir some chopped pecans into tuna salad or sprinkle on top.

- To make quick and simple tea sandwiches, mix 3 ounces of cream cheese with a tablespoon of milk or cream, then add ¼ cup chopped pecans and 2 tablespoons chutney or tart preserves.
- Spice up a plate of sautéed scallops with herbs, lemon juice and chopped pecans.
- Remember that pecans and cheese have a natural affinity for one another. Don't forget pecans on a cheese tray.

Peppery Cheese Spread

This spread is delicious as a snack or appetizer on crackers, but it can also be made into sandwiches. I like to use Pepperidge Farm's very thin white sandwich bread. For teatime, cut the sandwiches into small triangles or "fingers."

2 cups (8 ounces) shredded sharp Cheddar
   cheese *or* pepper Jack
½ cup mayonnaise
½ cup finely chopped pecans
¼ cup diced pimientos *or* sweet red pepper

2 teaspoons dried *or* minced fresh chives
¼ teaspoon freshly ground black pepper
Hot pepper sauce *or* minced jalapeños to taste
Crackers of your choice

In a bowl, combine the cheese, mayonnaise, pecans, pimientos, chives, pepper and pepper sauce; mix well. Serve with crackers.

Yield: about 2½ cups

33

Four-Cheese Pecan Pizza

This dish proves again that pecans work anywhere. It'll serve four to six people as an appetizer or two to three for lunch ... pumpkin soup would be a nice luncheon complement. Using a purchased pizza crust saves time, but you can make your own pizza dough if you prefer.

1 tube (10 ounces) refrigerated pizza crust
2 tablespoons pecan oil *or* olive oil, *divided*
2 large onions, sliced
1 package (3 ounces) cream cheese, softened
¼ cup goat cheese, softened
½ cup crumbled feta *or* blue cheese
1 cup (4 ounces) shredded mozzarella cheese
¾ cup pecan pieces
½ cup minced fresh parsley

34

Preheat oven to 450°. Unroll pizza crust onto a 12-inch pizza pan. Brush with 1 tablespoon oil. Place in oven for 3 minutes (to prevent a soggy dough). Remove from the oven and set aside.

In a large skillet, heat remaining oil. Cook onions over low heat until caramelized, about 20 minutes, stirring occasionally. Combine cream cheese and goat cheese; spread over prepared crust. Top with the onions, feta cheese, mozzarella cheese and pecans. Bake for 5–7 minutes or until cheeses are melted and top is lightly browned. Sprinkle with parsley. Serve hot.

Yield: 6-8 slices

After-Holiday Ham Biscuits

Around holiday time, when there is leftover ham in the house, these tiny meat pies are a good way to make new use of "old" ham.

2 cups finely chopped cooked ham
5 to 6 tablespoons butter, melted
1 tablespoon mayonnaise
1 teaspoon Dijon mustard
3 tablespoons shortening
2 cups self-rising flour
⅔ cup milk
⅓ cup finely chopped pecans

Preheat oven to 375°. In a small bowl, combine the ham, butter, mayonnaise and mustard; set aside. In a mixing bowl, mix shortening with flour. Gradually add milk and pecans, mixing with a fork. Knead briefly; roll out on a floured surface to about ⅛-inch thickness.

Cut dough into small rounds. Spread the ham mixture on half of the rounds; top with remaining rounds and seal the edges with the tines of a fork. Place on an ungreased baking sheet. Bake for 10 minutes or until golden brown. Serve hot.

Yield: 2 dozen

35

Spice-Up-the-Party Ham Spread

Here's another great way to use leftover holiday ham. Serve on crackers, or for lunch, spread on toasted pita rounds and top with a dollop of sour cream.

1 pound cooked ham (about 3 cups)
½ cup mayonnaise
¼ cup Dijon mustard
⅓ cup finely chopped pecans
1 tablespoon sweet pickle relish, optional

½ teaspoon Worcestershire sauce
⅛ to ¼ teaspoon prepared horseradish
⅛ to ¼ teaspoon hot pepper sauce

Grind the ham in a food processor. Add the remaining ingredients; process until combined. Transfer to a bowl; refrigerate for at least 30 minutes before serving.

Yield: about 3 cups

SALADS
Before, During and After

In times past, a salad was distinguishable from an entrée. We knew we were eating a salad because it was placed to the upper left of our dinner plate before or during the meal, or it came with cheese after the main course and before dessert.

Today, all that has changed, and frequently we dine on what is called an "entrée salad"—a term that usually means there is meat or a lot of cheese in the dish. Warm steak salad is popular as an entrée, as are chicken or shrimp Caesars.

With the fusion of foods of many cultures offered on our menus, we often find rice noodles in our salads, not to mention fruit, eggs, fish and fried wontons. This development is all to the good, especially if we remember to add pecans and seeds to salads that our forebears probably would have scoffed at.

The importance of fiber and leafy green vegetables in our diets has been well documented, and salads can go far to reduce our intake of empty calories in processed foods. Freshness and variety are ours when we choose salad greens of different kinds and insist on quality in our produce.

Simple Vinaigrette

The basic proportion for classic vinaigrette is a 3–1 ratio of oil to vinegar or lemon juice. This formula still holds true in most cases, and improving on it would be difficult indeed. The following mixture would go well with most salad greens. Choose lemon juice or vinegar depending on your menu.

6 tablespoons pecan oil *or* olive oil
2 tablespoons lemon juice, red wine vinegar *or* champagne vinegar
Salt and pepper to taste

In a bowl, whisk the oil and lemon juice or vinegar to form an emulsion. Season with salt and pepper.

Yield: ½ cup

Variations: Add fresh or dried herbs of your choice, or Dijon mustard, fresh garlic or garlic powder in small amounts.

By adding 1 tablespoon each of sour cream and buttermilk, you can turn this vinaigrette into a ranch dressing.

37

Simple Salad

For lunch, this salad is good with a hard-boiled egg or piece of cheese and tuna fish, canned or fresh.

Simple Vinaigrette (recipe above)
1 head Boston *or* butter lettuce, torn into bite-size pieces
1 perfectly ripe tomato, cut into thin slices
2 stalks hearts of palm (available in jars or cans), cut into nickel-size rounds
Freshly ground black pepper
¼ cup pecan pieces, toasted if desired

Make the vinaigrette with lemon juice. On salad plates, arrange the lettuce, tomato and hearts of palm. Add a few grinds of pepper and sprinkle with pecans. Drizzle with desired amount of vinaigrette; serve immediately.

Yield: 2-3 servings

Sensation Salad

In the 1950s and '60s, two brothers named Bob and Jake Staples owned a popular restaurant in Baton Rouge, Louisiana. Predictably, they named it Bob and Jake's, and it became a successful steak and seafood establishment. Jake had been a well-known football player, and the patrons enjoyed shaking his hand as he greeted them at the entrance.

Very few guests ate at Bob and Jake's without ordering a Sensation Salad, despite the fact that the aroma of garlic lingered on the breath long after the meal ended. It predated by decades (at least in the South) the ubiquitous Caesar Salad. As with a Caesar, this salad goes well with steak, seafood or heavy soups like gumbos or stews.

Dressing
1 cup vegetable oil
1 cup pecan oil or olive oil
Juice of 2 large lemons
4 large cloves garlic, minced
3 tablespoons white wine vinegar
8 ounces good-quality Romano or Parmigiano-
   Reggiano cheese, grated

Salad
1 large head romaine, torn into bite-size pieces
1 bunch fresh Italian or curly-leaf parsley,
   coarsely chopped
⅓ cup pecan pieces, toasted

In a quart jar with a tight-fitting lid, combine the dressing ingredients; shake until well blended. Store in the refrigerator until needed. Mixture will separate, so shake vigorously before dressing the salad.

In a large salad bowl, combine the romaine, parsley and pecans. Pour a generous amount of dressing over the salad; toss and serve immediately. Refrigerate remaining dressing for future use.

Yield: 4-6 servings
     (about 3 cups dressing)

Variation: To make an entrée salad, add shrimp or chicken tenders and increase the amount of greens.

39

Super Salad

Nuts are one of the 12 so-called "Super Foods," and the federal government recommends we consume at least nine of these foods daily. Spinach and broccoli are two more ... so this salad is not only good, it's good for you!

Dressing
Simple Vinaigrette (recipe on page 37)
1 tablespoon buttermilk
1 tablespoon mayonnaise
½ cup crumbled blue cheese, Gorgonzola *or* feta cheese

Salad
2 cups fresh spinach, stems removed and torn *or* baby spinach
1 cup torn arugula *or* other greens
1 cup fresh broccoli florets *or* cauliflowerets
4 green bell pepper rings
4 red bell pepper rings
½ onion, cut into thin slices
½ cup dried black beans, cooked *or* canned black beans
½ cup sliced carrots
¼ cup sliced fresh mushrooms
2 tomatoes, sliced *or* 12 grape tomatoes
½ cup pecan pieces, toasted

Make vinaigrette with lemon juice. Whisk in the buttermilk and mayonnaise; stir in the cheese. In a large bowl, toss the first 10 salad ingredients. Pour dressing over salad and toss again. Sprinkle with pecans; serve immediately.

Yield: 4 servings

Variation: To make an entrée salad, top with grilled salmon, shrimp or chicken. Otherwise, it's a compatible side salad with those same entrées.

Homemade Dressings Are Healthful

Another advantage of eating salads is the absence of sugar-filled calories. Thus, adding much sugar to a salad dressing would defeat the goal of healthy eating. Take care to read the label on store-bought dressings, since sugar is often a significant ingredient, and learn to make a few dressings that can be served with any number of salads.

Wintertime Relief Salad

During the winter, we feel the need for colorful, fruity salads that remind us of summer's fresh melons and peaches. This recipe meets that requirement, with mangoes both in the salad and in the creamy dressing. Luckily, we can get good mangoes in the off-season, as they travel well from their far-flung homes.

¼ cup rice vinegar *or* fruit-flavored vinegar

5 tablespoons pecan oil *or* olive oil

2 tablespoons honey

1 teaspoon dried *or* minced fresh chives

2 large *or* 4 small ripe mangoes, peeled and sliced, *divided*

1 head red *or* green leaf lettuce, torn into bite-size pieces

2½ cups torn arugula

¾ cup watercress leaves

2 ripe avocados, peeled and sliced

½ cup thinly sliced radicchio *or* Belgian endive

½ cup Candied Gingered Pecans (recipe on page 28)

For dressing, in a food processor, combine the vinegar, oil, honey, chives and ½ cup sliced mango; cover and process until blended. In a large bowl, combine the lettuce, arugula, watercress, avocados and radicchio or endive. Pour dressing over salad and toss to coat. Divide among individual plates; top each with pecans and remaining mango slices.

Yield: 8 servings

Variations: Add some sliced fresh strawberries to the salad, or substitute strawberries for mango in the dressing.

Instead of the candied pecans, substitute another roasted pecan recipe from the Starters chapter (pages 21–23 and 28) or plain toasted pecan pieces.

In summer, when fresh herbs are readily available, substitute 3 tablespoons of basil or mint for the radicchio or endive.

42

Fifties Lettuce Wedge Updated

Many of us remember the old-fashioned lettuce wedge salad from the 1950s. At the time, there was an orange-colored bottled dressing that drowned an unsuspecting quarter head of iceberg lettuce. Despite its popularity, that dish went out of style. Now lettuce wedges are coming back, but this time, the dressings aren't necessarily bottled, and they're certainly not that neon-orange color. The worth of this salad comes from the richness of the dressing and the quality of the lettuce.

Dressing from Super Salad (recipe on page 40)
1 head iceberg lettuce, quartered into wedges
Toasted pecan pieces

Make the dressing. Place lettuce wedges on salad plates. Just before serving, pour about ¼ cup dressing over each. Sprinkle with pecans.

Yield: 4 servings

Variations: Crumble blue cheese, Gorgonzola or feta on top of each wedge (whichever cheese you'd used in the dressing).

Use the dressing from the Sensation Salad (recipe on page 39) and add a few sprigs of fresh parsley on top.

During holiday time, sprinkle wedge with pomegranate seeds to add color and texture.

43

Salad of Baby Mesclun Greens

Mesclun is a popular mixture of baby greens, often including arugula, mâche, radicchio, frisée, mizuna, sorrel, dandelion and oak leaf lettuce. The young and tender leaves still carry a tartness of flavor. Since the flavor is stronger than Boston lettuce, the salad can take a more full-bodied dressing, thus the addition of Dijon mustard.

Simple Vinaigrette (recipe on page 37)
1 teaspoon Dijon mustard

3 cups baby mesclun greens
¼ cup pecan pieces, toasted if desired

Make the vinaigrette with lemon juice; whisk in mustard. Arrange greens on salad plates or place in a salad bowl; sprinkle with pecans. Drizzle with desired amount of vinaigrette; serve immediately.

Yield: 3-4 servings

Fruity Greens and Pecans

A nice salad for fall and winter, this mixture goes well with an entrée of meat, chicken or fish. It can also stand on its own as a luncheon dish, perhaps with a bowl of pumpkin or tomato soup. Use red or green pears or a combination of both.

Dressing
¼ cup pear nectar *or* orange juice
2 tablespoons pecan oil *or* olive oil
2 tablespoons white wine vinegar
1 teaspoon Dijon mustard
⅛ teaspoon ground ginger
⅛ teaspoon ground black pepper
Salad
10 cups mesclun *or* other greens, torn into
   bite-size pieces
3 ripe pears, each cut into eight slices

½ cup clementine *or* satsuma orange slices
½ cup pecan pieces, toasted *or* Candied
   Gingered Pecans (recipe on page 28)
½ cup crumbled blue cheese *or* shredded
   cheddar cheese
2 tablespoons roasted salted pepitas
   (pumpkin seeds)

In a jar with a tight-fitting lid, combine the dressing ingredients; shake well. For the salad, either combine the greens, pears, oranges, pecans and cheese in a large bowl, or arrange those ingredients on individual plates or a large platter. Drizzle with dressing and sprinkle with pepitas.

Yield: 8 servings

44

Packaged Greens Are Convenient

Many salad greens today are washed and prepackaged. This is a convenience, especially for the busy cook; however, you must check to be sure of freshness. In some markets, baby greens, mesclun mix and more are available in bulk in a large bin, presumably washed and fresh. It is important to pick over the supply and get only the best leaves. Whether purchased in bulk or packages, washing lettuces before using is recommended.

Wilted Spinach Salad

Salads with wilted greens have a long history. Our great-grandparents heated bacon drippings, added a little vinegar, salt and pepper and used the mixture as a warm dressing for salad greens as well as a topping for baked potatoes. This recipe calls to mind that cooking tradition.

3 to 4 bacon strips, diced
¼ cup apple cider vinegar
2 teaspoons sugar
½ teaspoon dry mustard
6 cups fresh spinach, stems removed and torn
   or baby spinach
1 cup sliced fresh mushrooms
¼ cup thinly sliced green onions
⅓ cup pecan pieces, toasted
1 hard-cooked egg, chopped*
Freshly ground black pepper, optional

In a large skillet, cook bacon until crisp; remove to paper towels. Reserve 2 tablespoons drippings. In a small bowl, combine the vinegar, sugar and mustard. Warm the drippings over medium heat; add vinegar mixture and bring to a boil.

Remove skillet from the heat. Add spinach, mushrooms and green onions; toss to coat. Divide mixture among salad plates; top with bacon, pecans and egg. Sprinkle with pepper if desired.

Yield: 4 servings

45

*If you have a Mouli grater, it works well for chopping the hard-cooked egg into small pieces.

In a Nutshell

The best method for cracking a whole pecan? Hold two in-shell pecans in the palm of your hand and squeeze, thereby cracking at least one of the nuts, sometimes both.

46

Waldorf with Roast Turkey

Waldorf salad has been on the list of comfort foods for years. This recipe offers a new twist, with the addition of raw fennel and toasted pecans, plus turkey to make it an entrée salad. For the greens, I suggest a mixture of red leaf, romaine and Boston or Bibb.

Dressing
½ cup mayonnaise
½ cup sour cream *or* plain yogurt
Juice and zest of 1 lemon
2 tablespoons orange juice
1 tablespoon pecan oil *or* light olive oil
½ teaspoon salt
¼ teaspoon freshly ground black pepper
¼ teaspoon freshly grated nutmeg
¼ teaspoon ground ginger
¼ teaspoon curry powder, optional

Salad
2 cups diced roast turkey (preferably breast meat)
1 large apple, peeled if desired, cored and diced
⅔ cup coarsely chopped pecans, toasted
½ cup dried cherries, cranberries *or* raisins, optional
¼ medium fennel bulb, diced
6 cups torn mixed salad greens
Orange *or* tangerine zest, green grapes *or* small blue cheese wedges, optional

For dressing, in a bowl, whisk the mayonnaise and sour cream until well blended. Add the lemon juice and zest, orange juice and oil; blend well with a whisk. Add seasonings and test for taste; adjust as needed.

In a large bowl, combine the turkey, apple, pecans, dried fruit if desired and fennel. Divide the salad greens among individual dinner plates or place on a large serving platter. Pour dressing over turkey mixture and toss to mix; spoon over greens. Garnish with orange zest, grapes or blue cheese if desired.

Yield: 4-6 servings

Variation: Substitute roast chicken for the turkey and celery for the fennel bulb.

In a Nutshell

Crushed pecan shells make good mulch in flower beds.

47

Festive Wild Rice-Pecan Salad

This salad conjures up thoughts of good times around a table laden with dishes of game, roasted meats or fowl. Its deep flavor and dark color suggest a winter's day with a roaring fire in the fireplace, and friends and family eating close by.

2 tablespoons chopped onion
2 tablespoons chopped celery
2 tablespoons butter
1 cup uncooked wild rice
3 cups chicken, beef *or* vegetable broth
2 tablespoons whiskey *or* bourbon, optional
Salt to taste
¾ dried cranberries *and/or* cherries
¼ cup chopped green onions
¼ cup minced fresh parsley
¾ cup coarsely chopped pecans, toasted
½ cup roasted salted pepitas (pumpkin seeds) *or* sunflower seeds
Dressing
⅓ cup pecan oil *or* olive oil
3 tablespoons cranberry sauce *or* cranberry chutney, warmed
2 tablespoons lime juice
2 tablespoons orange juice
1 teaspoon orange zest
1 teaspoon garlic powder *or* minced fresh garlic
Salt and pepper to taste

48

In a large saucepan, sauté onion and celery in butter. Add rice, broth, whiskey if desired and salt. Cover and cook over medium heat until level of liquid is even with rice. Reduce heat to low; cook 40 minutes longer or until tender, without stirring.

In a large bowl, combine the rice, cranberries, green onions, parsley, pecans and pepitas. Combine the dressing ingredients; pour over salad and toss. Serve warm or at room temperature.

Yield: 6-8 servings

Variations: This salad is a good way to use leftover wild rice from a holiday dinner. Or you can substitute a packaged long grain and wild rice mix with seasonings for the plain wild rice; follow cooking directions on the box.

To add some zip to the dressing, use Jalapeño Cranberry Compote (recipe on page 145) instead of cranberry sauce or chutney.

To make an entrée salad, add leftover pork, game or fowl.

For a pretty presentation, serve the salad in lettuce cups.

49

Thai Chicken, Pecan and Mango Salad

This entrée salad is filling, tasty and a perfect example of the ways in which cross-cultural culinary traditions are enhancing our dining style. Unlike in times past, a wide variety of ethnic food products can now be found in larger grocery stores.

Dressing
¼ cup chicken broth
2 tablespoons soy sauce
2 tablespoons hoisin sauce
2 tablespoons pecan oil *or* olive oil
1 tablespoon creamy peanut butter
1 tablespoon sugar
3 cloves garlic, minced
2 teaspoons toasted sesame oil
2 teaspoons grated fresh gingerroot
1 teaspoon crushed red pepper flakes
Salad
4 ounces uncooked angel hair pasta
2 large ripe mangoes, peeled and sliced
2 cups cubed cooked chicken
2 cups chopped bok choy
⅓ cup pecan pieces, toasted, salted and
   chopped
¼ cup thinly sliced green onions

In a jar with a tight-fitting lid, combine the dressing ingredients; shake well. Let stand for at least 15 minutes for the flavors to blend. Meanwhile, cook the pasta according to package directions; drain.

Toss pasta with 3 tablespoons dressing; divide among dinner plates. Arrange mangoes around pasta; place chicken and bok choy on top. Drizzle with remaining dressing. Sprinkle with pecans and green onions.

Yield: 4 servings

In a Nutshell

Texas Desirable pecan halves were selected as the first and only fresh food to nourish astronauts on the Apollo 13 and Apollo 14 missions in the 1970s. After that, pecans continued to be used on other space flights. No other nut has earned this high nutritional honor.

—*North Carolina Pecan Growers Association*

ENTRÉES
Plain and Fancy

Truly there is no end to the adaptability of this nut. Strong enough in flavor to stand on their own, or subtle enough to be paired in countless ways, pecans come to the dining table in both plain and fancy incarnations. Regardless of which dishes they enhance, pecans add nutrition and promote healthy dining, not to mention rich flavor.

Pecans can be advantageously used in sautéing, broiling, grilling or baking. Added to sauces, they boost taste and texture. Looking at the list of entrées offered in this chapter, the reader should marvel at the presence of pork, lamb, beef, fish, seafood, chicken, turkey and game. From homey meat loaf to elegant oysters, there's something for all appetites.

Vegetarian entrées benefit greatly from the presence of pecans, too, such as manicotti stuffed with spinach and sprinkled with smoky nuts ... or penne in a cream sauce laced with nutmeg and nuts.

Each of these main dishes uses pecans equally well, whether the nuts be in, on or around the pièce de résistance ... whether the pecans are ground, in halves or pieces. What other ingredient, save salt and pepper, can boast that level of versatility?

Turkey-Pecan Meat Loaf

There's no need for bread or cracker fillers in this meat loaf. Ground pecans act as a binder and add flavor simultaneously. It's a sumptuous dinner dish served hot, or an interesting luncheon dish when served at room temperature with a salad and/or soup.

½ medium onion, diced

1 small carrot, shredded

1 rib celery, diced

½ cup chopped fresh flat-leaf parsley

⅓ cup shredded peeled sweet potato, optional

1 clove garlic, minced

1 egg, beaten

1 tablespoon minced fresh thyme *or* 1 teaspoon dried thyme

1 tablespoon minced fresh rosemary *or* 1 teaspoon dried rosemary, crushed

Salt and freshly ground black pepper to taste

1 pound ground turkey breast

½ cup pecan pieces, toasted and ground

½ cup canned tomatoes with Italian spices *or* jalapeños, optional

2 thick slices uncooked bacon *or* pancetta

Preheat oven to 350°. In a large bowl, combine the onion, carrot, celery, parsley, sweet potato if desired, garlic, egg and seasonings. Crumble turkey over mixture and mix well. Add pecans and mix just until incorporated. Shape into an oval loaf; place in an ungreased 8-inch square baking dish.

Pour tomatoes over the top if desired. Place bacon or pancetta over loaf. Bake for 50–60 minutes or until a meat thermometer reads 165°. Let stand for 15 minutes before serving.

53

Yield: 4-6 servings

Variation: For added texture and flavor, add ⅓ cup cooked flavored rice, such as curried rice, "dirty rice" or wild rice, to the turkey mixture.

Oysters Escalope

Oysters and pecans, oddly, go together very well. This dish appears often at holiday time, as do oyster stew and oysters Rockefeller. Try the scalloped oysters as part of a buffet menu and watch them disappear. They're delicious served with champagne or a really good chilled white wine.

1 quart oysters
1 teaspoon salt
¼ teaspoon white pepper
1 tablespoon butter
2 cups coarse soda cracker crumbs
2 eggs
¾ cup milk
½ cup pecan pieces, roasted

54

Preheat oven to 350°. Remove any pieces of shell from oysters and place in a colander; pour boiling water over oysters. Place a layer of oysters in a greased 2-quart baking dish. Sprinkle with half of the salt and pepper; dot with butter. Add a layer of cracker crumbs. Repeat layers of oysters, salt, pepper and crumbs.

Beat the eggs and milk; carefully pour over crumb layer. Sprinkle with pecans. Bake, uncovered, for 20–30 minutes or until custard is set. Serve hot.

Yield: 6 servings

Crabmeat Au Gratin

Rich beyond words and needing no more than a salad and hot bread, this dish creates an unforgettable entrée. Champagne is the perfect accompaniment to complete a memorable dining experience.

2 tablespoons butter
1½ tablespoons all-purpose flour
½ teaspoon minced garlic
½ teaspoon salt
¼ teaspoon white pepper
1 cup milk
¼ teaspoon freshly grated nutmeg
⅛ teaspoon paprika
1 cup (4 ounces) shredded Havarti, Swiss *or* Gruyère cheese
2 cups lump crabmeat
¾ cup finely chopped pecans

In a Nutshell

Pecans are one of the largest fruit-bearing trees. One irrigated, managed acre of pecan trees will produce about 1,000 pounds of nuts.

Preheat oven to 300°. In a saucepan, melt butter over low heat. Slowly blend in flour, garlic, salt and pepper. Cook until smooth, stirring gently. Remove from the heat; gradually stir in milk. Add nutmeg, paprika and cheese. Return to low heat; cook until sauce is smooth and thickened.

Spoon 3–4 tablespoons of the cheese sauce into a greased 1½-quart baking dish; add crabmeat. Pour remaining sauce over the top; sprinkle with pecans. Bake, uncovered, for 15 minutes or until heated through.

Yield: 4 servings

Variations: To make individual servings, use four ramekins instead of one large baking dish.

For a good luncheon dish, serve the au gratin in baked puff pastry shells.

For brunch, serve the au gratin over scrambled eggs in pastry shells.

Shrimp Asparagus Mornay

A good brunch, luncheon or supper dish, the shrimp can be combined with or replaced by cubed chicken breast. It can be served on toast points, English muffins or herbed rice, or in crepes or puff pastry shells.

2 tablespoons butter
2 tablespoons all-purpose flour
1 cup milk
½ teaspoon freshly grated nutmeg
½ teaspoon salt
⅛ teaspoon white pepper
⅛ teaspoon cayenne pepper, optional
4 cups (1 pound) shredded Monterey Jack *or* Swiss cheese
½ cup finely chopped green onions
¼ pound fresh mushrooms, thinly sliced
2 cups cooked shrimp, peeled and deveined
2 pounds fresh asparagus, trimmed
½ cup pecan pieces, roasted

In a large saucepan, melt butter over low heat; stir in flour. Remove from the heat; gradually stir in milk, nutmeg, salt, pepper and cayenne if desired until smooth. Return to low heat; cook and stir until mixture attains the consistency of a sauce. Add cheese, a cup at a time, stirring after each addition until melted. Add onions, mushrooms and shrimp; stir gently until shrimp are coated and heated through.

Cook asparagus until crisp-tender. Top with shrimp mixture; sprinkle with pecans. Serve hot.

Yield: 6 servings

Variations: Replace a portion of the Monterey Jack or Swiss with grated Parmesan cheese.

Add 1 teaspoon of curry powder with the other seasonings.

For a bridal luncheon, baby shower or romantic dinner, add 1 tablespoon of tomato paste to achieve a pale pink color. With this addition, the sauce becomes more of a Nantua sauce.

Grilled Salmon with Pecan Butter

It is amazing that pecans pair so well with fish of various kinds. In this recipe, the salmon is done very simply and then flavored with a seasoned butter. Salmon fillets may be substituted for steaks. Lemon rice makes a nice side dish.

Pecan Butter
½ cup unsalted butter, softened
⅓ cup finely chopped pecans
1 tablespoon chopped fresh flat-leaf parsley *or* chives
1 tablespoon lemon zest
1 teaspoon lemon juice
2 teaspoons grated fresh gingerroot
¼ teaspoon salt
¼ teaspoon black pepper
Salmon
4 salmon steaks (6 ounces *each*)
1 tablespoon pecan oil *or* olive oil
1 teaspoon salt
1 teaspoon black pepper

In a small mixing bowl, combine the pecan butter ingredients; beat until well blended. Set aside.

Rub salmon steaks with oil and season with salt and pepper. Grill, broil or pan-sear for 4–5 minutes on each side or until salmon is cooked to desired doneness. Transfer to dinner plates or a serving platter; top each with a dollop of pecan butter. Pass the remaining butter.

Yield: 4 servings

Variation: The pecan butter may be formed into a log and chilled until firm, then cut into slices to top each piece of salmon.

59

Pecan-Encrusted Trout

This preparation also works well with salmon fillets. Serve the fish on a bed of pasta, or try cooked mustard greens or chard ... they go well with both the fish and the pecans. Instead of sautéing, you can broil the fillets if you prefer.

1 cup finely chopped pecans
½ cup dry breadcrumbs
1 teaspoon salt
1 teaspoon black pepper
4 trout fillets (6 to 8 ounces *each*)
¼ cup pecan oil *or* olive oil, *divided*
¼ cup butter

In a shallow bowl, combine the pecans, breadcrumbs, salt and pepper. Brush trout with 2 teaspoons oil; dredge in pecan mixture, turning to coat until well covered. In a large skillet, heat butter and remaining oil. Sauté trout for 4–5 minutes on each side or until fish flakes easily with a fork. Serve hot.

Yield: 4 servings

Pan-Sautéed Sole a la Beurre Pecane

At New Orleans' Galatoire's Restaurant, "Trout Amandine" has been a favorite item on the menu for more than 50 years. In this recipe, pecans replace the almonds to great advantage ... and we used sole for the photography session, since that was the freshest available. Use whatever fresh fish you can find, whether it's sole, trout or flounder.

½ cup all-purpose flour
1 teaspoon salt
½ teaspoon black pepper
1½ pounds fresh sole, trout *or* flounder fillets
¼ cup butter, *divided*
2 tablespoons pecan oil *or* olive oil
1 cup finely chopped pecans
Chopped fresh parsley

In a shallow dish, combine the flour, salt and pepper. Dredge the fillets. In a large skillet, heat 2 tablespoons butter; add oil. When skillet is hot but not smoking, sear the fillets on both sides, taking care not to tear the fish. Total cooking time should be no more than 5–7 minutes.

Remove fish and keep warm. Add remaining butter to pan juices. When hot but not smoking, add pecans and toss for 2 minutes to brown. Serve pan juices over fish; sprinkle with pecans and parsley.

Yield: 4 servings

61

Company Roast Chicken

This dish can take a range of side dishes—mixed wild and white rice, curried rice, potatoes au gratin or pasta. If using rice, spoon it around the chicken on the serving platter, using fruit and nuts for garnish. Red and green peppers make a colorful garnish at Christmastime.

When starting with a large roasting chicken, the promise of useful leftovers beckons. Cold chicken makes great salads and sandwiches. Heated, you can use it for tacos, combine with a pound of shrimp for gumbo or make a pasta dish with a cream sauce.

1 roasting chicken (5 to 7 pounds)
2 tablespoons pecan oil *or* olive oil
1 teaspoon salt
1 teaspoon black pepper
½ teaspoon garlic powder
½ orange, thickly sliced
½ white onion, thickly sliced
¼ cup pecan halves
¼ cup dried cranberries *or* cherries
3 sprigs fresh rosemary *or* thyme
3 sprigs fresh parsley
1 jalapeño pepper, optional
Fresh sweet *or* hot peppers and additional fruit, herbs and pecan halves for garnish

Preheat oven to 350°. Wash and clean chicken, removing giblets from cavity. Dry the chicken inside and out; rub with oil. Sprinkle salt, pepper and garlic powder inside cavity.

Squeeze the juice from the orange slices into the cavity; place rind inside. Add onion, pecans, cranberries, rosemary, parsley and jalapeño if desired, packing loosely.

Place chicken in a roasting pan. Bake, uncovered, for 1¾ to 2¾ hours or until a meat thermometer reads 180°. Cover and let stand for 10–15 minutes before carving. Garnish platter as desired.

Yield: 8-10 servings

Variation: When roasting fowl, don't forget Cornish game hens. Although their cavities are too small to add much fruit, the same flavor can be combined in an orange juice marinade. Pecans can garnish beautifully, and wild rice makes a superb side. Follow package directions for baking, and allow one hen per person.

62

Pecan-Encrusted Chicken Breasts

Before coating the chicken with flour and pecans, you can cut it into "fingers." This size is nice for children and is also better for serving on a salad. If using in a salad, be sure to add extra pecans to the greens!

½ cup milk
½ cup all-purpose flour
1 teaspoon salt
1 teaspoon black pepper
4 boneless skinless chicken breast halves (4 ounces *each)*
¾ cup ground pecans
½ cup pecan oil *or* olive oil
¼ cup butter

64

Pour milk into a shallow bowl. In another shallow bowl, combine the flour, salt and pepper. Dip chicken in milk, then dredge in flour mixture; dip again in milk, then coat with ground pecans until well covered. In a large skillet, heat oil and butter. Cook chicken over medium heat for 5–6 minutes on each side or until juices run clear (watching carefully so pecans don't burn). Serve hot.

Yield: 4 servings

Variations: Substitute 1 pound of catfish fillets for the chicken; prepare as directed.

When making fried chicken, grind about ¼ cup of pecans to almost a meal and add to flour after dipping the chicken pieces in milk or buttermilk. What flavor!

In a Nutshell

Pecan growers can identify nut varieties by looking across an orchard and noting the color of the trees' leaves. For example, Desirables have darker leaves than do the Schley variety.

Smothered Quail

This recipe uses a cooking method referred to as "smothering"—searing the quail to seal in the juices and then simmering them in liquid in a covered pot, allowing the meat to cook slowly and become tender. Toasted pecans add a delicious nutty flavor to the gravy.

½ cup plus 1 to 2 tablespoons all-purpose flour, *divided*

½ teaspoon salt

⅛ teaspoon black pepper

6 quail, dressed

½ cup plus 2 tablespoons butter, *divided*

3 tablespoons pecan oil *or* olive oil, *divided*

1½ cups boiling water

1 cup water

Hot pepper sauce and additional salt and black pepper to taste

⅓ cup pecan pieces, toasted

In a shallow bowl, combine ½ cup flour, salt and pepper. Dredge quail. In a large skillet, heat ½ cup butter and 2 tablespoons oil (being careful not to let oil smoke). Brown birds quickly to seal juices, turning often to brown on both sides. Reduce heat. Slowly add boiling water; cover and simmer for 25 minutes or until birds are tender and water has evaporated. Remove quail to a serving platter and keep warm.

For gravy, add remaining butter and oil to pan drippings in the skillet, stirring to loosen browned bits. Add remaining flour and stir gently (don't allow to burn). Slowly add water; season with pepper sauce, salt and pepper. Stir in pecans. Cook over low heat until thickened. Serve with quail.

65

Yield: 6 servings

Gourmet Roast Duck with Pecan Dressing

Most of these ingredients are grown in nature and are unprocessed. The ducks exist in the wild ... sometimes pecans do, as well—they are usually smaller than "improved" varieties, have a rich taste and are called "natives."

2 mallard *or* other wild ducks, dressed
1½ teaspoons salt
½ teaspoon black pepper
½ cup butter, melted
1 tablespoon pecan oil *or* olive oil
2 to 3 tablespoons lemon juice
6 sprigs fresh parsley
1 rib celery with leaves, cut into chunks
1 small onion, cut into wedges

Dressing
½ cup chopped onion
½ cup chopped celery
2 tablespoons butter
2 tablespoons pecan oil *or* olive oil
2 cups dried bread cubes
½ cup chopped pecans, toasted
½ cup dried cranberries, cherries *or* apricots
½ cup minced fresh parsley
½ teaspoon garlic powder
½ teaspoon black pepper
½ teaspoon dried thyme *or* rosemary, crushed
¾ cup giblet stock *or* chicken broth

Gravy
1 cup pan juices
½ cup orange juice
⅓ cup sherry *or* whiskey

Preheat oven to 325°. If giblet stock is desired, cook giblets in water for 30 minutes. Rub salt and pepper inside duck cavities. Combine butter, oil and lemon juice; brush inside cavities and over skin. Loosely stuff parsley, celery and onion into ducks; truss with string. Place in a roasting pan; tent with foil. Bake for 1½ hours.

Meanwhile, in a small skillet, sauté onion and celery in butter and oil. Transfer to a large bowl. Add bread cubes, pecans, dried fruit, seasonings and enough stock to moisten; toss to mix. Spoon into a greased 1½-quart baking dish. Cover and bake for 30 minutes.

Remove foil from ducks; baste with pan drippings. Bake 30 minutes longer or until browned. Uncover dressing; bake 10 minutes longer or until lightly browned. For gravy, transfer pan juices to a saucepan. Stir in orange juice and sherry; heat through. Remove and discard vegetables from inside ducks. Serve ducks and dressing with gravy.

Yield: 4-6 servings

66

Simply Wonderful Pork Tenderloin

Pork tenderloin has every advantage going for it: It's easy to prepare, is very versatile, as it can pair with many flavors, and is good hot or cold. All you need are two ingredients—the pork and soy sauce— for this basic, reliable preparation. In this recipe, the pork is served with ginger-chile dressing and lime-pecan rice.

Pork tenderloin can appear at a fancy dinner, be part of a buffet or go on a picnic with equal ease. In fact, it's like pecans—pork tenderloin is good anywhere, anytime. But unlike pecans, it cannot be eaten raw!

2 pork tenderloins (¾ to 1 pound *each*)
⅓ cup soy sauce
Ginger-Chile Dressing
Juice and zest of 1 lime
⅓ cup sugar
1 red chile pepper, cut into ¼-inch pieces
1 teaspoon grated fresh gingerroot
½ cup water
2 tablespoons pecan pieces, roasted
Lime-Pecan Rice
1 to 1½ cups uncooked long grain rice
⅓ cup pecan pieces, roasted
2 teaspoons lime zest

Preheat oven to 350°. Place tenderloins on a foil-covered baking sheet; pour soy sauce over meat. Bake for 50–60 minutes or until a meat thermometer reads 155°.

Meanwhile, combine the dressing ingredients in a small saucepan. Bring to a boil over medium-high heat; cook for 3 minutes. Cool to room temperature. Cook rice according to package directions; stir in pecans and lime zest. Let pork stand for 10 minutes before slicing into medallions. Serve with dressing and rice.

67

Yield: 6-8 servings
(about ½ cup dressing)

Variation: Instead of the lime-pecan rice, serve the pork with orzo pasta tossed with Something-Different Pecan Pesto (recipe on page 144).

In a Nutshell

Annual production of pecan nuts is about 1 pound for every citizen of the United States.
—*North Carolina Pecan Growers Association*

South-of-the-Border Pork Loin with Chipotle Mole

Here's another example of American cuisine being advantageously influenced by culinary traditions from other countries, featuring pork paired with Mexico's famous mole sauce. Serve with side dishes like guacamole, flour tortillas, refried beans, queso fresco, chopped tomatoes, sour cream and salsa.

68

1 boneless rolled pork loin roast (4½ to 5 pounds)
1 tablespoon pecan oil *or* olive oil
½ teaspoon salt
½ teaspoon black pepper
Mole Sauce
3 cloves garlic, minced
1 tablespoon pecan oil *or* olive oil
½ cup pecan pieces
1 cup canned plain tomatoes *or* tomatoes with jalapeños (including liquid)
1 slice whole wheat bread, toasted and torn into small pieces
3 to 4 chipotle peppers in adobo sauce
1 tablespoon unsweetened cocoa powder
1 tablespoon sugar
½ teaspoon ground cinnamon
¼ teaspoon ground cloves
¼ teaspoon black pepper
2½ cups chicken broth, *divided*

2 to 3 medium bananas, mashed
Additional pecan pieces, roasted

Preheat oven to 350°. In a Dutch oven, brown roast in oil on all sides for 10–12 minutes. Season with salt and pepper.

For sauce, in a skillet, sauté garlic in oil. Add pecans and spread in a single layer; cook and stir for 2 minutes or until lightly browned. Transfer to a blender; add tomatoes, bread, chipotle peppers, cocoa, sugar and spices. Cover and process until finely chopped and blended. Add ½ cup broth; process until mixture forms a paste. Pour into the skillet; add bananas and 1 cup broth. Simmer over low heat, stirring to avoid sticking, until sauce has the appearance of a cream soup. Pour over pork.

Add remaining broth to the Dutch oven. Bake, uncovered, for 1½ to 1¾ hours or until a meat thermometer reads 160°. Let stand for 10–15 minutes before slicing. Place on a serving platter with some of the mole sauce; sprinkle roasted pecans over entire dish. Pass the remaining sauce.

Yield: 10-12 servings

70

Chiles Rellenos en Nogada

Chiles rellenos appear on the menu in most Tex-Mex restaurants; however, this recipe takes them a step further with the addition of nuts. Of course, our version uses pecans!

Not as hot as jalapeños, yet still piquant, poblanos are large enough to be stuffed with a meat filling ... this filling is slightly sweet with the addition of raisins, banana and spices. The cool sauce can be served with roast pork and game as well.

When pomegranates are in season, the bright red seeds make this dish a colorful addition to a Christmas Eve buffet or other holiday meal.

2 slices day-old bread
¾ cup milk
½ cup finely chopped pecans
1 package (8 ounces) cream cheese, softened
1 tablespoon sugar
1 teaspoon ground cinnamon
Salt to taste
Stuffed Peppers
6 poblano peppers
1 pound ground beef *or* ½ pound *each* ground beef and pork
1 large tomato, diced *or* ⅔ cup diced canned tomatoes
1 tablespoon chopped onion
½ cup coarsely chopped pecans
½ cup raisins, soaked in water
½ cup shredded Monterey Jack cheese
½ banana, mashed, optional
½ teaspoon ground cinnamon
¼ teaspoon ground cloves
Salt to taste
Pomegranate seeds, optional

In a shallow bowl, soak bread in milk. Mix pecans and cream cheese; add to bread with sugar, cinnamon and salt. Chill until serving.

Preheat oven to 500°. Roast the peppers for 10–15 minutes, turning on all sides until blistered and blackened. Meanwhile, in a skillet, brown the meat. Add tomatoes and onion; sauté for 2–3 minutes. Stir in the pecans, raisins, cheese, banana if desired, cinnamon, cloves and salt; set aside.

Place peppers in a paper or plastic bag; let stand for 5–10 minutes. Reduce oven to 350°. Remove one pepper at a time and peel the charred skin; slit lengthwise and remove seeds. Carefully fill each pepper with meat mixture. Place on a baking sheet. Bake for 30 minutes or until heated through. Serve with chilled sauce. Sprinkle with pomegranate seeds if desired.

Yield: 6 servings

71

Pecan Grilled Steaks

Where pecans are grown, there are, of course, pecan trees. When winter storms or high winds force some branches to the ground, local "grillmeisters" race to collect them. Just as pecans add flavor to almost all foods, pecan wood imparts an unmistakable flavor to meat.

The broken or chopped up twigs and branches make an excellent outdoor grilling wood with a flavor milder than mesquite or hickory chips. Pecan wood is also good for grilling fish and seafood. If you don't have pecan trees where you live, look for the wood chips at barbecue supply stores and some gourmet groceries.

3 T-bone *or* rib-eye steaks (1 to 1½ inches thick)
Pecan oil *or* olive oil
Salt and freshly ground black pepper to taste
Pecan Butter (recipe on page 59)

Prepare your charcoal grill; add pecan wood chips when the coals are beginning to turn gray. Burn for a few minutes, allowing flame to subside. Lightly coat both sides of steaks with oil; season with salt and pepper. Place on the hot grill. Cook for 4–6 minutes on each side for medium-rare or until meat reaches desired doneness. Serve with pecan butter.

Yield: 6 servings

72

Lamb and Goats Together

Lamb chops and goat cheese with pecans—what a great combination! In springtime, I like to serve the lamb and mashed potatoes with early spring peas with tendrils when I can find them. Peas are sweet enough and need no additive except what the French do: Place a few leaves of Bibb or Boston lettuce in the bottom of a cooking pot, then cook peas briefly on top of the lettuce. Simply season with a little butter, salt and pepper—voilà!

73

Goat Cheese Mashed Potatoes

2 to 3 pounds baking potatoes, peeled and
   quartered
¼ to ½ cup milk
1 to 3 tablespoons butter
⅓ cup crumbled goat cheese
Salt and pepper to taste

Lamb Chops

¼ cup pecan oil *or* olive oil
12 lamb rib chops
1 tablespoon butter
¾ cup pecan pieces

Cook potatoes in boiling water until tender; drain. Mash with milk and butter. Stir in goat cheese; season with salt and pepper. Keep warm.

In a large skillet, heat oil. Sauté lamb chops for 3 minutes on each side or until meat reaches desired doneness. Meanwhile, in a small skillet, melt butter. Add pecans; cook and stir over low heat for 2–3 minutes.

Arrange lamb chops on a serving platter or individual plates; pour pecans and pan juices over meat. Serve with mashed potatoes.

Yield: 4-6 servings

Buffet Specials

When entertaining a large crowd with a buffet supper—be it friends, family or business associates—having a few reliable dishes to serve comes in handy. The following three recipes are good examples. With such hearty one-dish treats, the crowd can pass down the line to nibble the meat, weigh in on the salad and fill up on the pasta dishes. Again, these recipes can be plain or fancy, depending on what else is served during the meal.

Pasta with a Twist–Lemon, That Is

Most guests are pleased to stand in a buffet line if they can see a pasta dish waiting for them. The lemon zest adds lightness as a counterpoint to the cream. Lemon slices would make a pretty garnish and indicate the lemon flavor to follow.

8 ounces uncooked rotini pasta
2 cups cut fresh asparagus
1 cup thinly sliced zucchini *or* yellow summer
  squash
2 cloves garlic, minced
2 tablespoons butter *or* pecan oil
⅓ cup pecan pieces
½ cup heavy whipping cream *or* milk
1 tablespoon lemon zest
1 tablespoon diced pimientos, optional

Cook pasta according to package directions. Meanwhile, in a large skillet, sauté the asparagus, squash and garlic in butter or oil for 3 minutes or until vegetables are crisp-tender. Drain pasta. Using a slotted spoon, add vegetables to pasta; keep warm.

In the same skillet, sauté the pecans for 2 minutes; remove and set aside. Add cream and lemon zest to the skillet; bring to a boil. Boil for 2–3 minutes or until reduced to ⅓ cup. Pour over pasta; sprinkle with toasted pecans and pimientos if desired.

Yield: 4 servings

Variation: Add 2 cups of diced cooked chicken or ham, double the amount of sauce and omit the squash.

74

Spinach Manicotti with Smoky Pecans

Stuffed manicotti is a favorite dish for many Italians. Of course, almost any pasta dish is a favorite among Italians. Blessed with expert taste buds and the olive oil to go with them, Italians thrive on a Mediterranean diet. Sophia Loren once said, "Pasta never put an unattractive pound on me." We should all be so lucky!

8 uncooked manicotti *or* jumbo shells
¼ cup sliced green onions
1 clove garlic, minced
2 tablespoons pecan oil *or* olive oil
2 tablespoons all-purpose flour
1⅓ cups milk
3 ounces shredded pecorino *or* Swiss cheese
⅓ cup vegetable broth
1 egg, beaten
1 package (10 ounces) frozen chopped spinach,
   thawed and well drained
¾ cup ricotta cheese
½ cup grated Parmesan cheese
½ cup Smoky Roasted Pecans (recipe on
   page 23), chopped
1½ to 2 teaspoons freshly grated nutmeg
½ teaspoon lemon zest

Preheat oven to 350°. Cook manicotti according to package directions; drain and cool in a single layer of oiled foil. For sauce, in a saucepan, sauté onions and garlic in oil. Stir in flour until smooth. Add milk; cook and stir until thickened. Add cheese and stir until melted. Set aside.

For filling, in a mixing bowl, combine the broth, egg, spinach, ricotta, Parmesan, pecans, nutmeg and lemon zest; mix until well blended (break up spinach to avoid lumps). Spoon into manicotti shells; place in a greased baking dish. Pour sauce over shells. Cover and bake for 30–35 minutes or until bubbly and heated through. Best served hot.

Yield: 4 servings

In a Nutshell

To cover up a scratch on wooden furniture, try breaking a pecan half into two pieces and rubbing the uneven end across the "ding."

76

Perfect Penne
with Chard and Goat Cheese

Penne pasta is good to use with a creamy sauce, as its shape allows the sauce to adhere to it. Delicious coated in a Gorgonzola sauce or served with a spicy meat sauce, penne delivers flavor. Almost any type of greens goes with penne as well. In this recipe, chard adds vitamins and color, and pecans top it off with nutty flavor.

1 pound green *or* red chard
1 pound uncooked penne pasta
3 tablespoons pecan oil *or* olive oil, *divided*
1 large red onion, thinly sliced
⅛ teaspoon crushed red pepper flakes
2 cups small cherry tomatoes, stemmed
1 teaspoon salt
1 teaspoon black pepper
1 teaspoon garlic powder
1 cup pecan halves, roasted
1 log (5 to 8 ounces) goat cheese, crumbled

Preheat oven to 350°. Remove ribs from chard and cut into strips; set aside. Cook pasta according to package directions. Drain, reserving 1 cup of cooking water for sauce. Coat pasta with 1 teaspoon oil to keep it from sticking together; keep warm.

In a large skillet, sauté onion and pepper flakes in remaining oil for 3–5 minutes. Add chard; cover and cook until wilted. Add tomatoes; cook 2–3 minutes longer. Season with salt, pepper and garlic powder.

In a large bowl, combine the pasta, chard mixture and reserved cooking water. Add pecans and goat cheese. Stir to mix all ingredients and see how the dish makes its own creamy sauce! Serve hot.

Yield: 4-6 servings

77

SIDES
Off to the Left or
Directly in the Center

In today's dining pattern, side dishes can pose as a salad, an entrée, what used to be entremets or even a dessert. Often, restaurant diners will comment, "I'm going to have two appetizers instead of an entrée."

Then again, on occasion, as when thinking of risotto or a dressed-up baked potato, the diner will decide to order a side dish or two and a salad, omitting the entrée. Such a development does not reflect a financial consideration so much as implying the appeal of side dishes today.

In the past, a "side" was literally a small dish of green beans or coleslaw, but no more. Sides are now rich, delicious, filling and appealing. A side of spinach is more often a large bowl of creamed spinach that could serve as the main dish when paired with a side salad of cheese, fruit, prosciutto and greens.

Diners have the opportunity to read a long menu, ignoring the list of entrées, and plan a satisfying meal by ordering a salad, a side and a dessert if they want to. Conveniently for the health-conscious, pecans can and do appear in a variety of side dishes.

Sweet Potato-Broccoli Shepherd's Pie

This meatless dish pairs well with pork, chicken, fish or seafood. Accompanied by a bowl of soup, this recipe would be a nutritious luncheon treat. At dinner, it's a filling side.

2 pounds sweet potatoes *or* yams, baked and peeled

1 teaspoon grated fresh gingerroot

½ teaspoon five-spice powder *or* curry powder

2 teaspoons salt, *divided*

½ teaspoon black pepper

1 egg white

4 cups fresh broccoli florets

1 tablespoon lemon juice

¼ cup pecan pieces, toasted *or* roasted

1¾ cups ricotta cheese

¼ cup buttermilk

1½ teaspoons minced fresh oregano *or* rosemary *or* ½ teaspoon dried oregano *or* rosemary, crushed

⅓ cup grated Parmigiano-Reggiano cheese

Preheat oven to 350°. In a mixing bowl, mash the sweet potatoes. Add ginger, five-spice powder and ½ teaspoon salt; mash with a fork until creamy. Season with pepper and mix in egg white. Steam broccoli for 5 minutes or until crisp-tender; toss with lemon juice and ½ teaspoon salt.

In a food processor, coarsely grind the pecans; remove and set aside. Place ricotta, buttermilk, oregano or rosemary and remaining salt in food processor; process until smooth, about 2 minutes.

Spread half of the sweet potatoes into a greased 1½-quart baking dish. Layer with half of the ricotta mixture and half of the broccoli; repeat layers. Cover with remaining sweet potatoes. Sprinkle with ground pecans and Parmigiano-Reggiano. Bake, uncovered, for 30–40 minutes or until heated through. Let stand for 15 minutes before serving.

79

Yield: 6 servings

Uptown Sweet Potato

Of all of nature's root vegetables, the sweet potato is one of the healthiest, most colorful and economical. Despite the fact that "gourmet" varieties are available in most produce departments, sweet potatoes are rarely expensive. What a bargain—health, economy and versatility— all in one potato.

Sweet potatoes make it onto the list of "Super Foods" for good reason: They are filled with beta-carotene, vitamins C and E, and have a lower glycemic index rating, thus helpful for avoiding insulin resistance.

The daily recommendation for beta-carotene intake is to eat at least one serving of sweet potatoes, yams or other beta-carotene-rich vegetables, such as carrots, pumpkin, butternut squash and orange bell peppers.

1 medium sweet potato *or* yam
½ teaspoon pecan oil *or* olive oil
1 teaspoon butter *or* to taste
1 teaspoon ground cinnamon
2 tablespoons pecan pieces, toasted *or* roasted

Preheat oven to 350°. Wash sweet potato and dry with paper towel. Rub oil over potato and pierce skin with a fork or sharp knife. Place on a baking pan or piece of foil. Bake for 50 minutes (longer for a larger potato) or until tender. Test for doneness by piercing skin at the widest spot for softness. Make a slash mark with knife tip and open as for a baked potato. Mash ends toward middle to loosen flesh; top with butter, cinnamon and pecans. Serve hot.

Yield: 1 serving

Variations: To speed the baking process, the sweet potato can be partially or totally prepared in the microwave. For best results, microwave the potato on high for 8 minutes, then finish in the oven for 8 minutes or until tender. Or microwave for about 10 minutes and it's ready to eat.

Here's a delicious way to use leftover baked sweet potatoes. Peel the potato, keeping the flesh intact. Cut lengthwise into about five slices. Pan-fry in 1 tablespoon pecan oil over high heat; a crisp "fringe" will form on the sides. Good enough for dessert!

82

Butternut Squash Risotto

Squash, sweet potatoes and pumpkin are interchangeable in many recipes—in baked goods, in soups and in this risotto. Likewise, pecans go well with all three. Add some bits of ham or shrimp, and you can turn this hearty side into an entrée.

2 to 3 cups vegetable broth, *divided*
1 to 2 tablespoons pecan oil *or* butter
½ cup pecan pieces
2 tablespoons minced shallot
12 fresh sage leaves, finely chopped
1 cup uncooked Arborio rice
1 cup mashed cooked butternut squash
½ teaspoon salt
½ teaspoon black pepper
½ cup grated Parmigiano-Reggiano *or* pecorino cheese
Minced fresh chives and roasted salted pepitas (pumpkin seeds)

In a small saucepan, heat broth and keep warm. In a large saucepan or skillet, heat oil or butter. Sauté pecans, shallot and sage for 2 minutes. Add rice; cook and stir for 2–3 minutes. Add ½ cup of heated broth; cook and stir until liquid is absorbed. Add squash, stirring to mix well.

Continue to add broth, about ½ cup at a time, stirring after each addition to let mixture absorb liquid. The entire process should take 25–30 minutes. Risotto is done when it is creamy in consistency and the rice grains are still distinct.

Season with salt and pepper; taste and adjust if needed. Just before serving, sprinkle with cheese. Garnish with chives and pepitas.

83

Yield: 4 servings

Variations: Substitute sweet potatoes or pumpkin for the squash.

For a delightful garnish, fry additional sage leaves in hot pecan oil for less than 10 seconds.

Instead of grating the cheese ahead of time, bring a chunk to the table along with an Italian-type grater and let your guests grate their own.

"Chived" and "Pecaned" Corn Cakes

In deference to Native Americans, who taught our Colonial forebears to use corn and pecans, I offer these delicious corn cakes as a tasty side dish. For an entrée, top them with a creamed shrimp or chicken mixture and pair with a green salad. Figure two cakes per person.

1 cup yellow cornmeal
1 cup boiling water
¼ cup milk
½ cup fresh, frozen *or* canned whole kernel corn
1 egg, beaten
2 tablespoons ground pecans
1 tablespoon snipped fresh chives *or* cilantro
2 tablespoons all-purpose flour
1½ teaspoons baking powder
1 teaspoon sugar, optional
½ teaspoon salt
3 tablespoons pecan oil *or* olive oil

84

In a mixing bowl, combine the cornmeal and boiling water, stirring until well blended (mixture will be stiff). Stir in milk until smooth. Add corn, egg, pecans and chives; mix until blended. Combine the flour, baking powder, sugar if desired and salt; add to cornmeal mixture and stir until incorporated.

Heat oil in a large skillet. Drop batter by large spoonfuls into hot oil. Cook for 1½ to 2 minutes on each side or until golden. (Do not crowd pan; cook in batches if necessary.) Serve warm.

Yield: 1 dozen

Variation: Corn cakes can be served like blinis—topped with a dollop of sour cream and sprinkling of chives ... or for a special occasion, top them with a spoonful of black caviar and serve with a glass of champagne.

In a Nutshell

"Acrid" best describes the scent of a torn pecan tree leaf. If a pecan lover is far from home and missing the familiar, that strong scent is remembered as a "fragrance."

Elegant Stuffed Acorn Squash

In further recognition of the culinary contributions made by the Native Americans, it is important to remember that they taught us to use squash, as well as corn, pecans, beans and many other homegrown staples in our diet.

These stuffed squash are filled with nutritious bulgur wheat, vegetables, fruit and nuts. They make a lovely presentation and are hearty enough to serve as a vegetarian entrée—serve one squash half per person for a side and two halves for an entrée.

4 to 6 acorn squash
1 tablespoon pecan oil *or* olive oil
Bulgur-Pecan Stuffing
½ cup dried cranberries *and/or* cherries
2 tablespoons whiskey *or* sherry
5 cups water *or* vegetable broth
1½ teaspoons salt, *divided*
2½ cups bulgur
2 medium onions, diced
2 green onions, chopped
2 to 3 ribs celery with leaves, chopped
2 teaspoons pecan oil *or* olive oil
2 pears *or* tart apples, cored and cubed
1 tablespoon minced fresh basil *or* 1 teaspoon
    dried basil
1 cup coarsely chopped pecans, toasted

Preheat oven to 325°. Cut squash in half; scoop out pulp and seeds. Put halves back together. Coat with oil. Place in a baking dish; add about ½ inch of water. Bake, uncovered, for 25 minutes.

Meanwhile, place dried fruit in a small bowl; add whiskey or sherry. Set aside to soak for 30 minutes. In a medium saucepan, bring water or broth and ½ teaspoon salt to a boil. Add bulgur; cover and cook for 15 minutes or until all of the liquid has been absorbed.

In a large skillet, sauté the onions and celery in oil until tender. Add pears or apples and basil; sauté 2–3 minutes longer. Transfer to a large bowl; stir in the pecans and remaining salt. Drain the plumped fruit; add to vegetable mixture. Add bulgur and mix gently.

Increase heat to 350°. When squash and stuffing are cooled to room temperature, lay out both halves of each squash; pack stuffing into cavities. Place in a roasting pan. Add about ½ inch of water to pan. Cover with foil. Bake for 1 hour or until the sides of the squash can be easily pierced with a sharp knifepoint.

Yield: 4-6 servings

85

Roasted Vegetable Medley

While colorful leaves brighten the countryside, this dish adds interest to the fall table. A mix of potatoes, vegetables, mushrooms and nuts, the recipe allows the cook total freedom. It also allows flexibility when planning the entrée. This "autumn special" goes with almost anything, especially a pork roast or beef pot roast. Talk about comfort food!

86

1 large sweet potato *or* yam (about 10 ounces), peeled and cut into 1-inch cubes
1 large fennel bulb (about 1 pound), trimmed and cut into 8 wedges
1 small eggplant, cut into 1-inch cubes
1 zucchini, cut into chunks
8 ounces cauliflower, broken into florets
8 ounces small red potatoes, quartered
6 ounces mushrooms, halved
4 large shallots, peeled and quartered
½ cup pecan halves
1 to 2 sprigs fresh rosemary
2 to 3 tablespoons pecan oil *or* olive oil
1 teaspoon salt
1 teaspoon black pepper
2 tablespoons balsamic vinegar, *divided*

Preheat oven to 425°. In a large baking dish or roasting pan, combine the first 13 ingredients; stir in 1 tablespoon balsamic vinegar. Bake, uncovered, for 30–35 minutes or until slightly browned and tender, stirring every 10 minutes. Sprinkle with the remaining vinegar. Serve warm.

Yield: 4-6 servings

Variation: During the food photography sessions, a delicious soup came about accidentally. We had some leftover roasted vegetables along with leftover roasted butternut squash from the risotto (recipe on page 83).

Running out of refrigerator space, in desperation, we combined all those leftovers with some chicken broth and seasonings. Lo and behold, we created a wonderful new soup of a beautiful deep-orange color (once the cooled mixture was pulsed in the food processor). The pecans added an unexpected "crunch" that was delightful.

Top this nutritious warmed soup with a dollop of sour cream and a sprinkle of pepitas and voilà! You've got a dish fit for your fanciest guest or your most demanding family member.

Grits Good Enough for Mardi Gras

For years, grits have had a bad reputation outside the southern United States—stemming from the poor way they were often prepared, then served as a tasteless pool of runny pablum in a breakfast cafeteria line.

Properly cooked grits are good. Superbly prepared grits are, well, superb. To be used as an accompaniment to eggs and bacon, the cereal must be cooked the proper amount of time. The directions on the box will usually produce a worthy dish. Of course, as with any other food, adept seasoning—the right amount of salt, pepper and butter—helps enormously.

In this recipe, which can be served for brunch or even dinner, grits are used as a vehicle for garlic, cheese and pecans. In New Orleans, "Grits and Grillades" greets many revelers at private parties, especially during Mardi Gras. That dish features garlic-cheese grits served with round steak smothered in a rich, dark gravy.

3 tablespoons pecan oil *or* butter, *divided*
2 cloves garlic, minced
2 cups water *or* vegetable broth
½ cup quick-cooking grits (preferably yellow grits)
1 egg
1½ cups (6 ounces) shredded fontina *or* sharp Cheddar cheese, *divided*
½ cup coarsely chopped pecans
Additional coarsely chopped pecans, optional

89

Preheat oven to 325°. In a saucepan, heat 1 tablespoon oil or butter. Sauté garlic for 1 minute. Add water or broth; bring to a boil. Add grits slowly, stirring constantly. In a small bowl, beat the egg; stir in about ½ cup hot grits mixture. Return all to the saucepan, stirring constantly. Remove from the heat; stir in 1 cup of cheese, pecans and remaining oil or butter.

Spoon into a greased 1-quart baking dish; sprinkle with remaining cheese. Bake, uncovered, for 25–30 minutes or until a knife inserted near the center comes out clean. Let stand for 5 minutes before serving. Sprinkle with additional pecans if desired.

Yield: 4-6 servings

Toasted Polenta-Cheese Slices

Many people who consider grits a scourge tout polenta as a gourmet dish. Both originate in a cornfield and basically have much the same taste, depending on the treatment. The seasoning of grits and cornmeal make all the difference in the public outlook. Given time, the world might be willing to let grits into the corncrib fold, since it has already admitted polenta!

Polenta can be served with almost any meat, chicken, fish or seafood. It has been popular in Italy for centuries. To its credit, polenta is little more than what the early American Colonists called cornmeal mush, taken a step further. The masses eat it wherever corn is grown.

1½ cups (6 ounces) shredded fontina *or* mozzarella cheese
½ cup grated Parmesan *or* Romano cheese
2 tablespoons minced fresh basil *or* 2 teaspoons dried basil
2½ cups water
1 cup yellow cornmeal *or* quick-cooking polenta
1 cup cold water
½ teaspoon salt
½ cup coarsely chopped pecans, toasted

In a small bowl, combine cheeses and basil; set aside. In a saucepan, bring water to a boil. In another bowl, stir together cornmeal, cold water and salt; mix well. Slowly add to the boiling water, stirring constantly. Cook and stir until mixture returns to a boil. Reduce heat to low; cook until very thick, stirring occasionally.

Pour a third of the mixture into a greased 9-inch x 5-inch x 3-inch loaf pan. Sprinkle with a third of the reserved cheese mixture. Repeat layers, finishing with a layer of cheese. Cool for 1 hour; cover and chill overnight or for at least 6 hours. (This is a good dish to make ahead to this point.)

Cut polenta into slices; broil until toasted and browned. Top with pecans.

Yield: 6-8 servings

Variation: For a fun presentation, cut the polenta slices into triangles. Instead of broiling, lightly pan-fry in pecan oil or butter; brown the pecans at the same time, then drizzle the pan juices over the polenta and pecans when serving.

Pecan-Stuffed Mushroom Caps

This side dish can double as a first course or starter; allow about four caps per person. It's very satisfying—with a flavor like a poor man's escargot!

3 to 4 dozen white button mushrooms
1½ cups finely chopped pecans
½ cup chopped fresh parsley
½ cup unsalted butter, softened
3 cloves garlic, minced
1 teaspoon salt
1 teaspoon white pepper
1 teaspoon dried thyme
¼ cup heavy whipping cream, optional

Preheat oven to 350°. Remove stems from mushrooms and finely chop. Set aside 1½ cups for stuffing; save the remainder for another use. Place caps in a baking dish, hollow side up. In a mixing bowl, combine the pecans, parsley and reserved mushroom stems. Add butter, garlic, salt, pepper and thyme; mix until well incorporated. Stuff into mushroom caps. Drizzle with cream if desired. Bake, uncovered, for 20 minutes or until browned. Serve hot.

Yield: 3-4 dozen

Pecan Lore ... Some Sellers Weren't Always Sincere

Pecans have always been sold by the pound. In times past, when woodstoves were in popular use, some unscrupulous pecan sellers would weight down their 100-pound bags of nuts by inserting a length of round stovepipe in the center of each sack. They'd fill the pipe with rocks and the area outside the pipe with pecans.

When the stovepipe was removed, the pecans filled in to hide the "ballast." Thus, the unsuspecting purchaser would leave, having paid for useless rocks rather than 100 pounds of the nuts he had bargained for in good faith.

However, pecan growers did not invent dishonest sales tactics. According to legend, some stonecutters in ancient Rome were said to cover a mistake with wax. So the honest stonecutters adopted the phrase *sine cera*—"without wax"—to advertise their wares, giving definition to the English word "sincere."

Spruced-Up Brussels Sprouts

Brussels sprouts are a little like broccoli—you either like them a lot or not at all. It's like the difference between polenta and grits: Polenta and broccoli get better press. A member of the cabbage family, this vegetable is among the few that originated in Northern Europe. Brussels sprouts are so named because they were said to have been cultivated in 16th-century Belgium.

It's not as if Brussels sprouts are bad for us; it's just that no one has tried very hard to spruce them up and make them more appealing. They just sit there on a plate. This recipe should help win over a few followers.

⅓ cup sun-dried tomatoes (not packed in oil)
1½ pounds fresh Brussels sprouts
2 tablespoons pecan oil *or* butter
1 cup chopped onion
⅓ cup pecan pieces, toasted
1 teaspoon salt
½ teaspoon black pepper

Place tomatoes in a small bowl and cover with boiling water; let stand until softened.

Trim stems off Brussels sprouts, removing any wilted outer leaves. Cut the larger sprouts in half and leave the smaller ones whole.

In a skillet, heat oil or butter; sauté onion until translucent. Add sprouts; cover and cook until tender but not mushy, about 10 minutes. Uncover and cook 2 minutes longer. Season with salt and pepper. Drain the tomatoes if necessary. Toss the sprouts with tomatoes and pecans.

Yield: about 8 servings

93

Kohlrabi for the Novice

Kohlrabi gets its name from the German "kohl" (cabbage) plus "rabi" (turnip). More similar in taste to the turnip, only sweeter and not as strong, kohlrabi has kept its German name regardless of where it grows. It's too bad that this vegetable is not so popular globally, as it grows very easily. Even in wartime gardens it was so prolific, the growers got tired of it.

Kohlrabi's bulblike root grows underground. Some varieties have purple bulbs, but the white one (which actually looks pale green) is the most popular in the States. Here, pecans and honey accentuate the vegetable's flavor.

94

4 small kohlrabies (about 1 pound)
½ cup shredded carrot
2 tablespoons honey
2 tablespoons coarsely chopped pecans, toasted
1 tablespoon lemon juice
¼ teaspoon lemon zest
1 tablespoon snipped fresh chives
1 tablespoon butter

Peel the kohlrabies, removing the woody outside fiber with a sharp knife. Cut the flesh into ¼-inch strips. Bring a large saucepan of water to a boil; add kohlrabi strips and carrot. Cook for 5 minutes or until tender. Meanwhile, in a small bowl, combine the honey, pecans, lemon juice, zest and chives. Drain vegetables and place in a serving bowl; top with honey mixture and butter.

Yield: 4 servings

Dilled Petite Pois Avec Les Pecanes

Roughly translated, the name of this recipe is "little peas with pecans." Peas don't have the "bad rap" that burdens Brussels sprouts, but they can also be the butt of jokes. Some politicians, who are frequently called on to speak at luncheons and dinners, say they're on the "Chicken and Peas Circuit."

Many of us grew up on canned peas and hated them. One lady I know says they smelled like "wet dogs" when she opened the can. At a meal, she would intone, "Pass the 'wet dogs,' please." Just to be mannerly, she would serve herself about six little olive-green peas!

Fresh peas are available today, and the frozen varieties are tasty. As with any vegetable, the secret to success is proper cooking. To be at their best, peas should be almost al dente. Mushy peas gave peas a bad name. As the joke goes, "Mu shu pork is good; mushy peas are not!"

¼ cup chopped onion

1 tablespoon butter

2 cups fresh green peas, shelled *or* 1 package (10 ounces) frozen petite peas

2 teaspoons snipped fresh dill *or* ½ teaspoon dill weed

½ teaspoon salt

½ teaspoon black pepper

¼ cup pecan pieces, toasted

In a small skillet, sauté onion lightly in butter. Meanwhile, in a saucepan, bring 2 cups of water to a boil. Add peas; cover and cook over medium heat for 2–3 minutes or until crisp-tender. Drain in a colander and return peas to the pan. Add onion, dill, salt and pepper; toss. Sprinkle with pecans and serve.

95

Yield: 4 servings

Variation: This recipe can be prepared in the microwave. Place peas in a microwave-safe dish; cover and cook on high for 3 minutes or until crisp-tender. Then toss with the onion and seasonings as directed. (If using fresh peas, microwave with 1–2 tablespoons water.)

In a Nutshell

When stored, a shelled pecan's worst enemy is heat and light. Keep them cool!

BREAD BASKET
Biscuits, Muffins and More

Is bread still the "staff of life" ... and does a "light as a feather" biscuit still matter? What about huge muffins that mainline sugar first thing in the morning? Should fiber-filled cereal replace all of these old breakfast standbys?

In deciding what to eat, we have choices. We know to cut down on the sugar and increase the fiber in our diets. Those steps improve the benefits we get from our food intake. We can also consider how to *add* to our consumption as well as how to *eliminate* from it. Eating smaller portions of more nutritious foods is a good place to start.

Breads can include a lot of nutrition. In most cases, it isn't necessary to completely omit carbohydrates from our diets. But it is essential to good health that the carbs we do take into our bodies are not carriers of empty calories. That's where pecans come in!

Most of the recipes in this chapter include at least one of the 12 "Super Foods" (always pecans!)—then it could be oats, sweet potatoes, nuts, chocolate or blueberries. (The other seven on the list are black beans or lentils, salmon, spinach or other leafy greens, broccoli, tomatoes, soy and onions.)

Comforting Cinnamon Toast with a Pecan Twist

When it comes to comfort food, what could be better than cinnamon toast, that beloved treat from our childhood? In our best memories, our mother was in the kitchen when we came home from school, eagerly asking, "How about some cinnamon toast?"

In an ideal world, the butter was straight from the creamery and the bread was homemade. Sure, and we had gotten all A's on our report cards, too! Cinnamon toast is a worthy treat for rewarding a good report card, be it in first grade or grad school—or a course in Learning in Retirement.

2 slices good white bread, crusts removed
2 teaspoons butter
2 teaspoons sugar
1 teaspoon ground cinnamon
1 tablespoon finely chopped pecans

Turn oven to Broil (or use a countertop toaster oven). Spread bread with butter. Combine sugar, cinnamon and pecans; spread evenly over bread. Broil until butter melts and starts to bubble or brown, being careful not to burn. Remove from oven and cut each slice into four "fingers." Good with milk, tea, coffee or hot chocolate, depending on age of celebrant!

97

Yield: 8 toast fingers

In a Nutshell

Georgia pecan wood was selected by the Atlanta Olympic Committee to make the handles of the torches for the 1996 Olympic Games. The torches were carried in the 15,000-mile trek across the USA and in the lighting of the Olympic flame in Atlanta on July 19, 1996.

—*Georgia Pecan Commission*

98

Puff Pastry Pecan-Cinnamon Rolls

These treats taste like something from a fine bakery. Children love helping with this recipe, as it is fast-moving and oh, so good! For a family of four, thaw just one puff pastry sheet and cut the other ingredients in half. Or make the whole batch and save some rolls for another day.

1 package (17.3 ounces) frozen puff pastry
    sheets, thawed
1 cup sugar
4 teaspoons ground cinnamon
⅓ cup coarsely chopped pecans
Confectioners' Sugar Icing
1½ cups confectioners' sugar
2 tablespoons butter, softened
2 tablespoons milk
1 teaspoon vanilla extract

Preheat oven to 400°. Unfold pastry sheets. Combine sugar and cinnamon; sprinkle over pastry. Sprinkle with pecans. Roll up each pastry jelly-roll style, starting with a long side.

(Hold the dough firmly and roll tightly so the dough does not sag.) Pinch seam to seal. With a sharp knife, cut the dough into ½-inch to ¾-inch slices. Place on an ungreased baking sheet. Bake for 10–15 minutes.

Combine the icing ingredients until smooth; drizzle or spread over rolls.

99

Yield: 16-20 rolls

Variation: Instead of icing, serve cinnamon rolls with Honey Pecan Butter (recipe on page 140).

In a Nutshell

Pecan trees usually range in height from 70 to 100 feet, but some trees grow as tall as 150 feet or higher. Native pecan trees—those over 150 years old—have trunks more than 3 feet in diameter.

—*North Carolina Pecan Growers Association*

Mother's Day Morning Cinnamon Rolls

Here's a perfect recipe for children to make on the Saturday before Mother's Day. Those younger than 8 will need assistance … and those under 13 will need supervision using the oven. Children of any age will love surprising their moms with a treat this delicious!

12 frozen white dinner rolls (unbaked dough)
½ cup packed brown sugar
1 package (3½ ounces) cook-and-serve
  butterscotch pudding mix
½ cup chopped pecans
⅓ cup raisins
2 teaspoons ground cinnamon
½ cup butter, melted

Arrange the frozen rolls in a Bundt pan. In a bowl, combine the brown sugar, pudding mix, pecans, raisins and cinnamon; sprinkle over rolls. Pour butter over the top. Cover and let rise in a warm place overnight until doubled in size. (Tell Mom not to peek!)

The next morning, preheat oven to 350°. Bake rolls for 30 minutes. Carefully invert pan onto a serving platter and serve warm.

Yield: 1 dozen

Easy Honey-Nut Toast

No one should be too busy in the morning to indulge himself with this treat. Keep a nutritious loaf of your favorite bread on hand and toast it while you're looking for the car keys!

2 slices good bread
½ teaspoon butter, optional
1 teaspoon ground cinnamon *or* apple pie spice
2 tablespoons honey
2 tablespoons pecan pieces

Turn oven to Broil (or use a countertop toaster oven). Spread bread with butter if desired; toast. Sprinkle with cinnamon or apple pie spice. Spread honey evenly over bread; top with pecans. Toast until honey is bubbly and pecans are toasted.

Yield: 1-2 servings

Quick Biscuit Fold-Overs

Some mornings are just too busy to make a breakfast treat from scratch. Fortunately, today's supermarkets offer a multitude of "helpers" that can be adapted to quick use. Here, see how refrigerated biscuits are easily transformed into a special treat.

2 tubes (12 ounces *each*) refrigerated biscuits
½ cup butter, melted
1 cup sugar
4 teaspoons ground cinnamon
⅓ cup coarsely chopped pecans
2 teaspoons orange zest

Preheat oven to 400°. Separate biscuits; roll out each biscuit to enlarge and flatten slightly. Place butter in a shallow bowl. Combine the sugar and cinnamon in another bowl. Sprinkle pecans and orange zest evenly over biscuits; fold dough over to encase filling and press edges to seal. Dip in butter, then roll in cinnamon-sugar. Place on an ungreased baking sheet. Bake for 8–11 minutes.

Yield: 20 biscuits

101

Variation: Substitute refrigerated crescent rolls for the biscuits; sprinkle cinnamon-sugar, pecans and orange zest over each triangle. (Omit the butter.) Place 1 teaspoon apricot preserves at the wide end of triangle; roll up and place on an ungreased baking sheet. Bake according to package directions.

Muffin-Tin Ham Biscuits

These versatile biscuits can be served with eggs and grits for breakfast ... or make mini ones and serve with drinks in the evening. The mayonnaise replaces the usual shortening in a biscuit recipe. If making mini biscuits, chop the pecans very finely.

2 cups self-rising flour
2 cups diced country ham *or* regular baked ham
1 cup milk
½ cup mayonnaise
⅓ cup finely chopped pecans

Preheat oven to 425°. In a mixing bowl, combine all ingredients, stirring with a fork just until combined. Drop by spoonfuls into 12 greased muffin cups or 24 miniature muffin cups. Bake for 15 minutes (large) or 8–10 minutes (small) or until golden brown. Leftover muffins freeze well.

Yield: 1-2 dozen

Hearty Breakfast Biscuits

Although this recipe is not difficult, it takes a little more time than the first few recipes in this chapter. These biscuits offer a lot of nutrition, along with delicious flavor!

1¾ cups all-purpose flour

¼ cup unprocessed wheat bran *or* pecan meal

2 tablespoons sugar

1 tablespoon baking powder

½ teaspoon ground cinnamon

¼ teaspoon salt

½ cup cold butter *or* shortening

⅔ cup milk

½ cup dried fruit (dried cherries, cranberries *or* apricots, cut into small pieces)

⅓ cup finely chopped pecans

½ cup confectioners' sugar, optional

2 to 3 teaspoons orange juice *or* additional milk, optional

Preheat oven to 450°. In a mixing bowl, combine the first six ingredients. Cut in butter until mixture resembles coarse cornmeal. Make a well in the center; add milk, dried fruit and pecans. Stir with a fork just until blended and dry ingredients are moistened.

Turn dough onto a floured surface; knead just until smooth. Roll into a circle about ½ inch thick. Cut with a floured 2½-inch biscuit cutter. Place on an ungreased baking sheet. Bake for 10–12 minutes or until golden brown.

If icing is desired, combine confectioners' sugar and orange juice; drizzle over warm biscuits.

Yield: 1 dozen

103

In a Nutshell

Pecan wood is used in agricultural implements, baseball bats, hammer handles, furniture, wall paneling, flooring, religious carvings and firewood.

Muffins Six Ways

"Breakfast on the go" can still be nutritious. This recipe allows the addition of any number of healthy tidbits that also enhance the enjoyment of early morning. Baked in paper muffin liners, the muffins can go in the car, on the golf course or to the office. Take two—you may meet a hungry friend.

Muffins with Nothing but Pecans Added

1¾ cups all-purpose flour
⅓ cup sugar
2 teaspoons baking powder
½ teaspoon salt
1 egg, beaten
¾ cup milk
¼ cup pecan oil *or* vegetable oil
½ to 1 cup coarsely chopped pecans
Additional 2 teaspoons sugar, optional

Preheat oven to 400°. In a mixing bowl, combine the flour, sugar, baking powder and salt. Make a well in the center; add egg, milk and oil. Stir just until moistened. Fold in pecans (batter will be lumpy).

Fill greased or paper-lined muffin cups two-thirds full. Sprinkle with additional sugar if desired. Bake for 12–20 minutes or until lightly browned. Serve warm if possible.

Yield: about 1 dozen jumbo muffins, 1½ to 2 dozen regular muffins or 3 dozen mini muffins

104

South-of-the-Border Cheese Muffins

Add ¼ teaspoon chipotle chili powder to the dry ingredients; fold in ½ cup shredded Monterey Jack cheese with the pecans. Serve with scrambled eggs; add salsa to the eggs to taste, and serve with sour cream, guacamole and extra salsa. For a late-morning breakfast or brunch, well-seasoned black beans are another good accompaniment.

Sweet Potato or Pumpkin Muffins

Add 1 teaspoon ground cinnamon, ½ teaspoon freshly grated nutmeg and ⅛ teaspoon ground cloves to the dry ingredients. Reduce milk to ½ cup and add 1 cup mashed sweet potato or pumpkin to the wet ingredients. Fold in 1 cup raisins if desired. (Paper liners are not recommended with this variation.)

Cranberry Muffins

Add 2 tablespoons sugar to the dry ingredients; fold in 1 cup coarsely chopped cranberries with the pecans.

Cherry-Apricot Muffins

Fold in ½ cup dried cherries and ½ cup dried apricots, cut into small pieces, with the pecans.

Date-Pecan Muffins

Add 1 tablespoon orange juice and 1 teaspoon orange zest with the wet ingredients; fold in ½ cup chopped dates with the pecans.

Healthy Pecan-Bran Muffins

Not only are these muffins nutritious, the batter can be kept in the refrigerator for 6 weeks without losing quality—so this recipe is a real "keeper." Mix the batter, bake what you need and save the rest for another time ... you can have freshly baked muffins at the drop of a hat. And with the suggested variations, you can make the muffins different each time you use the batter.

6 cups bran cereal (not flakes), *divided*
2 cups boiling water
1 cup pecan oil *or* vegetable oil
3 cups sugar
4 eggs, beaten
1 quart buttermilk
¾ cup finely chopped pecans
5 cups whole-wheat flour *or* all-purpose flour
5 tablespoons baking soda
2 teaspoons salt
½ to 1 cup flax seed meal, optional

Preheat oven to 400°. Place 2 cups bran in a bowl; add boiling water. Let stand for 5 minutes; stir in oil. In another bowl, combine the sugar, eggs buttermilk, pecans and remaining bran. Stir in bran/oil mixture.

Sift the flour, baking soda and salt into a mixing bowl; add flax seed meal if desired. Make a well in the center; stir in wet ingredients just until moistened. Fill desired amount of greased muffin cups. Bake for 20–25 minutes. Store any unused batter in the refrigerator for up to 6 weeks.

Yield: 6 dozen

Variations: Use half whole-wheat flour and half all-purpose flour (2½ cups of each).

Sprinkle sunflower kernels or roasted salted pepitas (pumpkin seeds) over muffin batter before baking.

Cornbread with Cheese and Jalapeños

Spice up an old-time favorite by adding cheese and jalapeños—and pecans, of course! You can also use this cornbread for a spicy, tasty dressing for turkey or other game ... it makes about 8 cups of crumbled bread.

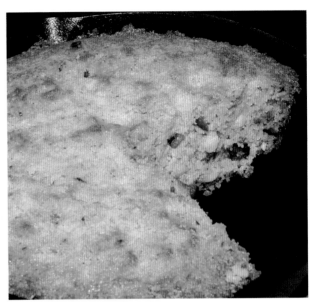

2 tablespoons pecan oil *or* vegetable oil

2 cups yellow cornmeal

1 tablespoon sugar

2 teaspoons baking soda

1 teaspoon salt

4 eggs, beaten

1 cup buttermilk

1 can (14¾ to 15 ounces) cream-style corn

1½ cups (6 ounces) shredded Monterey Jack cheese

2 to 4 tablespoons diced fresh *or* canned jalapeño peppers

¾ cup butter, melted

⅓ cup finely chopped pecans, toasted

Preheat oven to 375°. Spread oil into a 13-inch x 9-inch x 2-inch baking pan or ovenproof skillet; place in oven until hot (be careful not to burn). Meanwhile, in a mixing bowl, combine the cornmeal, sugar, baking soda and salt. Stir in eggs, buttermilk, corn, cheese and jalapeños. Add butter; stir just until blended.

Carefully remove pan from oven; pour batter into pan. Bake for 45 minutes or until golden brown. Cut into squares or desired shapes. Serve warm.

Yield: 8-12 servings

Variation: Use pepper Jack cheese and omit the jalapeños.

Meal-in-a-Loaf Earth Bread

This recipe produces a taste similar to the popular Morning Glory Muffins. The moist bread can be served warm or cold, and it keeps well. Try it and discover how nourishing and flavorful a loaf of bread can be!

⅓ cup dried figs, cut into small pieces
1 tablespoon rum, bourbon *or* fruit juice
3 eggs
2 cups sugar
1 teaspoon vanilla extract
2 cups whole-wheat flour
1 cup all-purpose flour
1 teaspoon salt
1 teaspoon baking soda
¾ teaspoon baking powder
¾ teaspoon pumpkin pie spice
¼ teaspoon ground cinnamon
1 cup shredded *or* grated zucchini
½ cup shredded *or* grated carrots
½ cup chopped pecans
½ cup mashed bananas
⅓ cup flaked coconut
2 tablespoons roasted salted pepitas
   (pumpkin seeds)

Preheat oven to 375°. In a small bowl, combine the figs and rum or juice; soak for 5 minutes. In a mixing bowl, combine the eggs, sugar and vanilla. Sift the dry ingredients together; add to egg mixture. Fold in the zucchini, carrots, pecans, bananas, coconut and figs.

Pour into one large greased loaf pan or two medium loaf pans; sprinkle with pepitas. Bake for 50–60 minutes or until a toothpick comes out clean.

Yield: 1-2 loaves

Variations: Substitute another type of dried fruit for the figs.

Instead of pumpkin pie spice, use a combination of ground nutmeg and cloves.

Substitute sweet potatoes for the zucchini.

Make muffins with the batter instead of loaves.

Ready-Mix Pancakes with Pecans

Pancakes and children go together. Pancakes and good times go together as well. Put all three components together, and you have an opportunity for creative cooking. Children as young as 3 years old can help mix up the batter, but they should not help with the actual cooking. Let them sit on the counter and watch, keeping a distance from the hot stove.

Today, most boxed pancake mixes result in a worthy product. Since they usually amount to a ready-made set of dry ingredients, all you need to do is add eggs and liquid. That's a real convenience, especially when cooking with and for children. Plus, with the extra time saved by not measuring out a list of ingredients, you have the luxury of experimenting with a few variations. Try those suggested at right, but not all at once!

2 cups biscuit/pancake mix
1 cup milk
2 eggs
⅓ cup finely chopped pecans
Pancake syrup *or* Honey Pecan Butter (recipe on page 140)

In a mixing bowl, combine the mix, milk and eggs just until blended (batter may be lumpy). Fold in pecans. Pour batter onto a lightly greased hot griddle or skillet; turn when bubbles form on top of pancakes. Serve with syrup or Honey Pecan Butter.

Yield: about 12 pancakes

Variations: Add ⅓ cup sliced or mashed bananas.

Add ⅓ cup blueberries (don't thaw if frozen).

Add ⅓ cup pumpkin purée or shredded peeled sweet potatoes.

Add ⅓ cup shredded apples.

110

In a Nutshell

The pecan is the state nut of Alabama, and the pecan tree is the state tree of Texas.

Made-from-Scratch Pecan Waffles

Waffles are another breakfast treat that young children love to be in on. Let them help mix the batter, but keep them away from the waffle iron. Put them in charge of telling you when the light comes on, while you pour yourself another cup of coffee or turn the bacon.

Like pancakes, good waffles can come from a box. So if you're in a hurry, try the variation. And for an extra-special treat, try serving the waffles with Honey Pecan Butter (recipe on page 140) instead of syrup.

2 cups all-purpose flour
3 teaspoons baking powder
1 teaspoon sugar
½ teaspoon salt
1½ cups milk
2 eggs, beaten
3 tablespoons pecan oil *or* melted butter
⅓ cup finely chopped pecans

In a mixing bowl, combine the flour, baking powder, sugar and salt. Combine the milk, eggs and oil or butter; stir into dry ingredients just until blended (batter may be lumpy). Fold in pecans. Bake in a preheated waffle iron according to manufacturer's directions.

111

Yield: about 8 waffles

Variation: To make waffles faster, combine 2 cups biscuit/pancake mix, 1⅓ cups milk and 2 tablespoons vegetable oil; fold in ⅓ cup finely chopped pecans. Bake in a preheated waffle iron according to manufacturer's directions.

Old-Fashioned Spoon Bread

Our grandmothers knew spoon bread much better than we do. They served it as a comforting, filling dish—a cross between a side dish and hot bread—at an evening meal. Often, the 19th-century diner would pour a little cane or maple syrup over his second portion of spoon bread, much the way people did with grits at that time.

We would all profit by bringing spoon bread back. But instead of syrup, why not accompany it with a dollop of Honey Pecan Butter?

112

1 cup yellow cornmeal

2½ cups water, *divided*

2 tablespoons pecan meal (see Source Guide on page 170)

1 teaspoon salt

1 cup milk *or* buttermilk

4 eggs, beaten

2 tablespoons pecan oil *or* melted butter

Honey Pecan Butter (recipe on page 140)

Preheat oven to 400°. Place cornmeal in a bowl; stir in ½ cup water (to prevent lumps). In a saucepan, bring remaining water to a boil. Slowly add the salt, pecan meal and cornmeal mixture, stirring constantly. Cook for 1 minute.

Remove from the heat. Beat in the milk, eggs and oil or butter until smooth. Pour into a greased or buttered 1½-quart baking dish. Bake for 40 minutes or until firm. Serve hot with Honey Pecan Butter.

Yield: 4-6 servings

Sally Lunn with Honey Pecan Butter

Legend has glamorized Sally Lunn, who, according to one tale, was a baker in 18th-century Bath, England. If you visit Bath today, you can take tea in the same tearoom where she is said to have made and sold her namesake bread. There, it's served as a round bun with clotted cream and various jams.

The basic recipe, modified here to include pecans, is used at Gadsby's Tavern in Alexandria, Virginia. It produces a large round loaf that is cut at the table into individual portions. Regardless of its origin, Sally Lunn bread is delicious!

¾ cup milk

½ cup shortening *or* pecan oil

1 package (¼ ounce) active dry yeast

¼ cup warm water (110° to 115°)

3¼ cups all-purpose flour

2 tablespoons pecan meal (see Source Guide on page 170)

¾ cup sugar

½ teaspoon salt

1 egg, beaten

Honey Pecan Butter (recipe on page 140)

In a saucepan, heat milk and shortening to the temperature of a baby bottle (wording of the old recipe!). In a small bowl, dissolve yeast in warm water. In a mixing bowl, combine flour, pecan meal, sugar and salt. Stir in warm milk mixture. Add egg and yeast mixture; beat until the dough comes off the sides of the bowl. Cover and let rise in a warm place until doubled in size, about 1½ hours.

Punch dough down; shape into a round loaf. Place on a greased baking sheet. Let rise until doubled, about 45 minutes. Preheat oven to 300°. Bake loaf for 30 minutes; brush with some Honey Pecan Butter. Bake 15 minutes longer or until loaf sounds hollow when lightly thumped in the center. Brush again with Honey Pecan Butter. Serve warm.

113

Yield: 1 loaf (2 pounds)

SWEET REVENGE
and Other Temptations

All sweets are not created equal. Some are easily passed over, while others are difficult to resist, but all can be consumed in small portions. The key is to be selective, saving a place in our days for a delicious morsel now and again.

It's no coincidence that where there is a nearly irresistible dish, whether sweet or savory, pecans often appear. Thanks to their versatility and delectability, they add to the enjoyment of appetizers, salads, entrées, side dishes, breads and condiments, as well as desserts. Of course, you'll find pecan pie in these pages, but I hope you'll find other intriguing sweet treats you'd like to try.

To gain a place in this chapter, a dessert had to offer such an enjoyment ratio that it was either worth the calories ... contained relatively fewer calories than most other desserts ... or could be made as a gift whose calories would be welcomed at a special occasion. In all cases, the recipes have been embraced by my family for more than one generation, sometimes for almost a century.

Some of these sweets can be prepared with and for children, and all are guaranteed to bring joy from the first bite to the last.

Lula Mae's Brown Sugar Pecan Pie

While there are several ways to make a high-quality pecan pie, this recipe was offered with an uncommon fervor. The lady named in the title had been a longtime family cook and rejected any other method for creating a delectable pie. While she's deceased, Lula Mae's pie lives on.

1 box (16 ounces) light brown sugar
3 tablespoons self-rising flour
6 tablespoons evaporated milk
3 eggs
½ cup butter, melted
2 teaspoons vanilla extract
2 teaspoons apple cider vinegar
1 teaspoon cornmeal
1 cup pecan pieces
1 unbaked pie shell (9 inches)

Preheat oven to 350°. In a mixing bowl, combine the brown sugar and flour. Add milk, eggs, butter, vanilla, vinegar and cornmeal; stir to blend. Spread pecans evenly in pie shell. Pour egg mixture over pecans. Bake for 1 hour or until set.

Yield: 8 servings

115

A "Food Epiphany"

A perfect illustration of being selective when enjoying sweets is the case of a friend who was having trouble dieting. At least she was having trouble until she had a "food epiphany"—she'd awakened in the night and sat up in bed, shocked to realize that *she* was in control of what she ate, *food* wasn't.

She knew at that moment of revelation that she could choose to eat or not eat any delectable item presented to her.

Sweets and corn chips had been her downfall, and she bravely declared sovereignty over them, choosing to eat no other sweets than pecan pralines...and fewer corn chips when she craved a salty treat. She met with weight-loss success by consuming only small amounts of her nemeses and doing so on rare occasions.

With that strategy, she didn't have to say "no" to temptation permanently. It would have been more difficult, if not impossible, for her to have never tasted her two favorite goodies again. Rationing was do-able.

Classic Pecan Pie

When Karo Corn Syrup first appeared on the market in 1902, it took the country by storm. Before that time, housewives had to take their empty syrup jugs to the grocery store to be filled. Cane syrup in the South and maple syrup in New England met certain market needs, and private makers had their own customers; but there were few convenient retail sources for individually bottled syrup.

The Corn Products Refining Company in New York and Chicago promoted Karo as "The Great Spread for Daily Bread." Children put it on waffles and pancakes, and mothers—who believed the syrup was rich in vitamins and a caloric asset— even added it to their babies' bottles.

The wife of one of the company's sales executives had the idea to expand the syrup's use. She concocted a mixture of eggs, sugar, Karo, butter and pecans— and the pecan pie, as we know it, was born.

Through the years, the recipe has changed little. Other versions, such as Bourbon Pecan Pie and Amaretto Pecan Pie, have come and gone. The original persists and appears on millions of holiday tables year after year, altered little since early in the 20th century.

3 eggs
1 cup sugar

1 cup Karo Dark Corn Syrup
2 tablespoons butter, melted
1 teaspoon vanilla extract
1½ cups pecan halves
1 unbaked deep-dish pie shell (9 inches)
Spiked Whipped Cream (optional)
1 cup heavy whipping cream
1 tablespoon bourbon *or* brandy
1 teaspoon vanilla extract

Preheat oven to 350°. In a mixing bowl, lightly beat the eggs. Whisk in the sugar. Add corn syrup, butter and vanilla; mix until well blended. Arrange pecan halves in the pie shell, distributing evenly.* Pour egg mixture over pecans. Bake for 55-60 minutes or until a knife comes out clean. Cool before slicing.

If whipped cream is desired: Whip cream in a mixing bowl until it begins to thicken. Add bourbon or brandy and vanilla; whip until cream forms stiff peaks. Serve with pie.

Yield: 8 servings

*Some methods suggest adding the pecans to the egg mixture before filling the pie shell. Pouring the mixture over the pecans creates a crisper texture that is preferred.

116

117

Nutty Meringues

Somewhat magical in their transformation from liquid egg whites into light, puffy confections, meringues are a good recipe for a child's first cooking lesson. Even a short attention span can be held as the beaters whip up the frothy mixture while the young cook spoons in the sugar.

That first whiff of pungent vanilla is unforgettable, especially compared to the astringent scent of the vinegar. In almost no time, the satiny substance is ready to be dipped up and baked. However, this recipe isn't a good one to make when stuck indoors on a rainy day—humidity is the enemy of meringues.

4 egg whites
Pinch salt
1 teaspoon white vinegar
¾ cup sugar
1 teaspoon vanilla *or* almond extract
2 tablespoons ground pecans

Place egg whites in a mixing bowl; let stand at room temperature for 30 minutes.

Line two baking sheets with parchment paper; set aside. Beat the egg whites until frothy. Add salt and vinegar. Gradually add sugar, 1 tablespoon at a time, beating on high until stiff glossy peaks form and sugar is dissolved. Beat in vanilla. Sprinkle pecans over mixture and fold in by hand.

Drop by tablespoonfuls 2 inches apart onto prepared baking sheets. Place in a cold oven and turn heat to 250°. Bake for 1 hour. Turn oven off; leave meringues in the oven for 2 hours. Store in an airtight container.

Yield: about 3 dozen

Variations: For chocolate meringues, add 1 tablespoon cocoa powder to the batter.

Use the same egg white batter (without the pecans) to make Pavlova, an Australian dessert named after a Russian ballerina. Drop batter into mounds and shape into cups with the back of a spoon. When baked and cooled, fill meringues with whipped cream and fresh fruit.

For a spectacular presentation, shape the egg white batter into one large ring, omitting the pecans. Fill the cooled meringue with vanilla or coffee ice cream, drizzle with hot fudge sauce and sprinkle with pecans. If that's not enough, also sprinkle with crushed Heath bars!

Pecan Meringue Pie with a Secret

Good enough for any adult gathering and simple enough for a child's second cooking lesson, this recipe will interest the group when everyone learns what's in it.

For at least 50 years, maybe even longer, there have been "mystery" recipes using Ritz crackers. First came the fake apple pie, which led people to say, "But it tastes just like apples!" Then came the secret pecan pie, for which the comment is simply, "It's so good!"

This recipe offers convenience, as it requires no pie shell; it forms its own. And the cook, young or old, can have fun playing "Betcha can't guess what's in this!"

3 egg whites
1 teaspoon baking powder
¾ to 1 cup sugar
1 cup chopped pecans
20 Ritz crackers, crushed
1 teaspoon vanilla extract
Whipped cream

Preheat oven to 350°. In a mixing bowl, beat egg whites until frothy. Add baking powder and beat to incorporate. Gradually add sugar, beating until stiff peaks form. Fold in pecans, cracker crumbs and vanilla. Pour into a greased 9-inch pie plate. Bake for 30 minutes. Cool before slicing. Serve with whipped cream.

119

Yield: 6-8 servings

Nameless Cake

¾ cup shortening

1½ cups sugar

3 eggs, beaten

1¾ cups all-purpose flour

½ teaspoon baking soda

½ teaspoon salt

¾ teaspoon ground nutmeg

1 teaspoon ground cinnamon

3 tablespoons cocoa powder

¾ cup buttermilk

1 to 2 teaspoons vanilla extract

½ cup chopped pecans, toasted

Nameless Icing

½ cup butter, softened

4 cups confectioners' sugar

3 tablespoons cocoa powder

1½ teaspoons ground cinnamon

2 tablespoons strong hot coffee

3 tablespoons milk *or* half-and-half cream

2 teaspoons vanilla extract

¾ cup pecan pieces *or* halves

120

Preheat oven to 350°. In a mixing bowl, cream shortening and sugar. Add eggs and blend. Sift dry ingredients together; add to creamed mixture alternately with buttermilk. Mix well. Blend in vanilla and pecans.

Pour into two greased 9-inch round cake pans, one 15-inch x 10-inch x 1-inch baking pan or 24 muffin cups. Bake for 24–33 minutes (for cakes) or 17–22 minutes (for cupcakes) or until a toothpick comes out clean. Cool completely.

For icing, in a mixing bowl, cream butter. Sift the confectioners' sugar, cocoa and cinnamon; add to butter alternately with coffee. Beat in milk and vanilla until well blended. If using pecan pieces, fold into icing and spread over cake. If using pecan halves, first ice the cake, then arrange pecans over icing.

Yield: 1 two-layer cake,
     1 sheet cake or
     about 2 dozen cupcakes

A number of stories abound as to the origin of this unusual cake. Family legend has the recipe appearing in a newspaper sometime in the 1930s, the result of a contest held by a flour company.

At the time, the mixture of chocolate, cinnamon and coffee flavors wowed the public, causing some to say the confection was too good to give an adequate name.

For over 70 years, it has served as a birthday cake, appeared at tailgate parties, gone on picnics and assisted in countless celebrations ... and has yet to be given a proper name. Now that mocha flavors have become de rigueur, the combination may not surprise, but it will continue to delight.

The original cake recipe contained a teaspoon of lemon extract. As the recipe was passed down in my family, it was omitted. A relative who was viewed as the arbiter of good taste suggested, during World War II, that lemon flavoring did not go with coffee and pecans. Apparently no one argued with that notion; for more than 60 years, there has been no lemon extract in the family Nameless Cake.

In addition, the 1930s icing recipe contained a raw egg yolk, which has also been omitted here with no detriment to the overall result.

121

Quick Pecan-Chocolate Mousse

Learning about transformation is interesting for children. Turning whipping cream into whipped cream is fun ... turning whipping cream into butter is not! Teach the child to hold the beaters low and keep them low (lest they cover themselves and the wall) and supervise the process to avoid failure. The trick is to not overbeat.

1 pint heavy whipping cream
¼ cup sugar, optional
1 cup chocolate syrup
12 homemade *or* purchased meringues
½ cup chopped pecans, toasted

In a mixing bowl, whip the cream. Add sugar if desired. Fold in the chocolate syrup. Refrigerate until chilled. To serve, crumble meringues into sundae dishes or stemmed wine glasses. Spoon mousse on top. Sprinkle with pecans.

Yield: 8 servings

Variations: If serving four or fewer people, divide all of the ingredients in half.

Omit the chocolate syrup and fold in berries or peaches.

Substitute shortbread cookies or brownies for the meringues.

122

Magic Cookie Bars

A pioneer in America's dairy business, Gail Borden invented a method for "evaporating" milk in order to prevent spoilage in 1854. By adding sugar to evaporated milk, he created what we know today as sweetened condensed milk. His business got a big boost during the Civil War when the Union army ordered it for use as a field ration.

Borden's "Elsie the Cow" made condensed milk a household name, and the company created many desserts using its product, printing the recipes inside the label on the can. Miniature "booklets" later appeared taped on top of each can, featuring new confections that consumers were eager to try.

The recipe for these rich, gooey bars is the Borden Eagle Brand's best-loved classic, pleasing crowds of any age. Children can easily help make these bars, layering the ingredients in the pan, but they will need adult supervision to put them in the oven.

½ cup butter
1½ cup graham cracker crumbs
1 can (14 ounces) sweetened condensed milk
2 cups (12 ounces) semisweet chocolate chips
1⅓ cups flaked coconut
1 cup chopped pecans

Preheat oven to 350° (325° for a glass dish). Place butter in a 13-inch x 9-inch x 2-inch baking pan; place in oven until melted. Sprinkle graham cracker crumbs evenly over butter. Pour milk over the crumbs. Layer with chocolate chips, coconut and pecans, distributing evenly. Bake for 25 minutes or until lightly browned. Cool before cutting.

123

Yield: 2-3 dozen

Variation: Replace 1 cup of semisweet chocolate chips with 1 cup butterscotch chips.

In a Nutshell

If a pecan pie is 9 inches in diameter, it would take 97,812,000 pecan pies to circle the Earth!

—Georgia Pecan Commission

"Millionaire's Delight" Chocolate Pound Cake

Although chocolate appears on the list of Super Foods, any chocoholic will tell you that isn't the reason many people require a "chocolate fix" now and again. The taste, texture and sensation it imparts cannot be provided by any other substance.

This cake keeps well and travels well. It can be enjoyed with a simple dusting of confectioners' sugar. It becomes even more delightful with the fudge-like icing on top. For a hot fudge sundae treat, top wedges of cake (iced or plain) with a scoop of vanilla or coffee ice cream and hot fudge sauce. Purchase hot fudge sauce or try "Gilding the Lily" Hot Fudge Sauce on the next page.

1 cup butter, softened
½ cup shortening
3 cups sugar
6 eggs
3 cups all-purpose flour
½ teaspoon salt
½ teaspoon baking powder
½ cup cocoa powder
1¼ cups milk
1 to 2 teaspoons vanilla extract
¼ cup finely chopped pecans

Chocolate Fix Icing
1 box (1 pound) confectioners' sugar
½ cup butter
6 heaping tablespoons evaporated milk, undiluted
6 heaping tablespoons cocoa powder
2 teaspoons instant coffee granules
3 teaspoons vanilla extract
½ cup pecan pieces *or* halves

Preheat oven to 300°. In a mixing bowl, cream butter, shortening and sugar. Add eggs, one at a time, beating after each addition. Sift dry ingredients together; add to creamed mixture alternately with milk. Mix well. Blend in vanilla and pecans.

Pour into a greased 9-inch Bundt or tube pan. Bake for 1 hour and 25 minutes.

When cake comes out of the oven, combine the first five icing ingredients in a large skillet over very low heat.

As the butter melts, stir to mix with the other ingredients. When combined and the mixture becomes satiny and workable, add vanilla and pecans; mix well (icing should be spreadable but not runny). Pour hot icing over cake while it is still warm.* Cool for 15 minutes before removing from pan to a serving plate.

Yield: 12-14 servings

*The purpose of heating the icing is not to cook it, but to melt the butter and just heat the mixture enough to make it easy to spread. It will harden to a nice texture when cool. If desired, prick holes in the top of the cake with the tines of a fork to allow the icing to seep inside.

The icing is versatile and can be used on sheet cakes and cupcakes of all flavors, but it might be tricky on layer cakes, as it is best poured while hot.

"Gilding the Lily" Hot Fudge Sauce

Chocolate and pecans are a perfect pairing, as you'll see in this delicious dessert topping. After one taste, you'll believe that "Too much of a good thing is—a good thing."

¼ unsweetened Dutch-process cocoa powder
⅓ cup packed dark brown sugar
½ cup light corn syrup
⅔ cup heavy whipping cream
¼ teaspoon salt
6 ounces high-quality bittersweet chocolate, finely chopped, *divided*
2 tablespoons unsalted butter, cut into 6 pieces
¼ cup finely chopped pecans
1 teaspoon vanilla extract

In a saucepan, stir together the cocoa, brown sugar, corn syrup, cream, salt and half of the bittersweet chocolate. Cook over medium heat, stirring until chocolate is melted. Bring to a low boil, stirring occasionally, for 5 minutes.

Remove from the heat; add the butter, pecans, vanilla and remaining chocolate. Stir until smooth. Cool slightly before serving. Store leftover sauce in an airtight container in the refrigerator for up to 1 week. Reheat over low heat, stirring to keep mixture well blended.

Yield: about 1½ cups

125

Key Lime Pie with a Pecan Twist

You needn't live in Florida to enjoy Key lime pie ... the juice is now available in a pint-size bottle in many supermarkets around the country. The tart lime flavor pairs well with the creamy richness of the condensed milk. The layer of pecans between the crust and filling seems to cut the sweetness of the pie, thus making it possible to eat a bigger slice!

1 can (14 ounces) sweetened condensed milk
3 egg yolks
½ cup bottled Key West lime juice
⅓ cup chopped pecans
1 ready-made graham cracker crust (9 inches)
1 cup heavy whipping cream

Preheat oven to 350°. In a mixing bowl, combine the milk and egg yolks until blended. Add lime juice and mix well. Set aside about 1 tablespoon of pecans for garnish. Sprinkle the remaining pecans evenly over crust; gently pour filling over pecans. Bake for 15 minutes. Cool.

Whip the cream until stiff; carefully spread over pie. Sprinkle with reserved pecans. Chill until serving. Store leftovers in the refrigerator for up to 3 days.

Yield: 6-8 servings

Pecan Lore ... Why Some Pecans Were Known as "Interstate Nuts"

When the Mahan variety of pecan was introduced, it was a large, attractive nut that looked very promising. A retail buyer would often purchase the Mahans based on their appearance. The wily seller knew the nuts looked better than they actually were and would price them at a lower rate, giving the appearance of a bargain.

The unsuspecting buyer gets in his car and drives a few miles, then decides to sample part of the booty. Feeling smug that he'd gotten the beautiful pecans at such a good price, he eagerly tears into the sack for a handful of fresh pecans.

Much to his surprise, he realizes he's bought a lot of inferior-tasting product ... and by this time, he's too far down the interstate to turn back for a refund!

Caramel Pecan Pie "Fix"

For those who aren't chocoholics, there's caramel and butterscotch. A friend once said when someone offered her a caramel apple, "Forget the apple—I'll be happy with the caramels!"

This luscious pie is the old-fashioned kind; you don't have to unwrap caramel candies to make the filling ... you start with caramelized sugar, butter, eggs and milk.

1 cup sugar, *divided*
¼ cup cornstarch
¼ teaspoon salt
2 cups milk
3 egg yolks
3 tablespoons butter
1½ teaspoons vanilla extract
¾ cup chopped pecans
1 deep-dish pie shell (9 inches), baked
Meringue
3 egg whites
½ teaspoon cream of tartar
1 teaspoon vanilla extract
3 tablespoons sugar

Preheat oven to 400°. Sprinkle ½ cup sugar into a heavy skillet. Cook over low heat, stirring constantly, until melted and light golden in color. Continue cooking, stirring constantly, until thickened and bubbly. Set aside.

In a saucepan, combine cornstarch, salt and remaining sugar; stir in milk until blended. Cook and stir over medium heat until mixture begins to thicken. In a bowl, beat the egg yolks. Stir about ½ cup of hot milk mixture into yolks; return all to the saucepan. Bring to a gentle boil; cook and stir 2 minutes longer. Add caramelized sugar and cook until thickened. Remove from the heat. Add butter, vanilla and pecans; stir to blend. Pour into pie shell.

For meringue, in a mixing bowl, beat egg whites, cream of tartar and vanilla until foamy. Gradually beat in sugar, 1 tablespoon at a time, until stiff peaks form and sugar is dissolved. Spread evenly over filling, sealing edges to crust. Bake for 10 minutes or until golden brown. Cool for 1 hour. Refrigerate for at least 3 hours before cutting.

Yield: 6-8 servings

128

Aunt Grace's Caramel Fudge

Most of the candy-eating world knows of the glories of chocolate fudge. This recipe could convert even the most extreme chocolate lover. My mother and her sister Grace kept a candy-making competition going for over 60 years. This fine cook insisted her caramel fudge was the winner, while my mother stuck to her praline entry (recipe on page 131).

4 cups sugar, *divided*
Pinch salt
1 cup milk
2 tablespoons light corn syrup
2 tablespoons butter
1½ teaspoons vanilla extract
3 cups chopped pecans

Butter a 13-inch x 9-inch x 2-inch pan; set aside. Sprinkle 1 cup sugar into a heavy skillet. Cook over low heat, stirring constantly, until melted and light golden in color. Continue cooking, stirring constantly, until thickened and bubbly. Set aside.

In a heavy saucepan, combine the salt and remaining sugar; stir in milk and corn syrup. Cook slowly, stirring constantly, until mixture boils. Add caramelized sugar and cook until mixture reaches the soft ball stage (234°–240° on a candy thermometer).*

When the ball forms, remove pan from the heat. Add butter, vanilla and pecans; stir until creamy. Pour into prepared pan; cool. Cut into squares or bite-size pieces. Store at room temperature.

Yield: 30-40 pieces

*Drop a teaspoon of the hot mixture into a cup of cold water. If it's ready, candy will form a soft "ball" when held between two fingers. More than one test may be required.

130

My Mother's Perfect Pecan Pralines

My family has treasured this recipe since 1928, when my mother (at age 12) cut it out of a newspaper. From that day to this, no one has veered from its directive; consequently, there have not been many faulty pralines in the family in more than 75 years!

While the recipe looks simple, calling for few ingredients, the tricky part comes in deciding when the mixture has achieved the "soft ball stage." With a candy thermometer, it's easier, but some purists refuse to use one. Practice makes perfect, and a good eye helps turn the creamy concoction into about 22 memorable morsels.

1 cup buttermilk
2 cups sugar
1 teaspoon baking soda
2 cups pecan halves
1 tablespoon butter
2 teaspoons vanilla extract

Place about 2½ feet of waxed paper on the kitchen counter. In a heavy saucepan, bring buttermilk and sugar to a boil, stirring constantly. Add baking soda very slowly (otherwise mixture will boil over the sides of the pan). Continue to cook and stir over medium heat for about 7 minutes (time varies; can take longer) or until mixture reaches the soft ball stage (234°–240° on a candy thermometer).*

When the ball forms, remove pan from the heat. Add pecans, butter and vanilla; stir until candy loses its high gloss and there is slight resistance against the spoon. Drop candy by spoonfuls onto waxed paper. As it cools, it will harden somewhat but remain creamy. Store at room temperature.

131

Yield: 22-24 (2-inch) pralines

*Drop a teaspoon of the hot mixture into a cup of cold water. If it's ready, candy will form a soft "ball" when held between two fingers. More than one test may be required.

"Marilyn Monroe" Brownies

Like chocolate fudge, brownies are known the world over. This "blonde" version, like the actress of the same name, is rich and voluptuous. The basic recipe comes from the repertoire of the late, great Helen Corbitt, founder and doyenne of the Zodiac Room at Neiman Marcus in Dallas. She both taught and lived by culinary example, bringing enjoyment to thousands of eager cooks who were searching for ways to entertain well.

Although out of print, her "Helen Corbitt Cooks for Company" from 1974 espouses good food attractively presented. If the book can be located on the Internet, it is a worthy addition to a cookbook collection.

4 tablespoons butter, melted
1 cup packed dark brown sugar
1 egg
¾ cup all-purpose flour
1 teaspoon baking powder
½ teaspoon salt
1 teaspoon vanilla extract
½ cup semisweet chocolate chips*
½ cup chopped pecans

Caramel Icing
½ cup butter
½ cup packed dark brown sugar
¼ cup milk *or* half-and-half cream
1¾ to 2 cups confectioners' sugar
1 teaspoon vanilla *or* maple extract

Preheat oven to 350°. In a mixing bowl, combine butter and brown sugar. Add egg and mix until blended. Combine the flour, baking powder and salt; add to egg mixture. Add vanilla, chocolate chips and pecans; stir to blend. Pour into a greased 8-inch square baking pan. Bake for 25 minutes. Cool.

For icing, in a small saucepan, melt butter until browned. Add brown sugar; cook and stir until sugar is completely melted. Stir in milk or cream. Remove from the heat; cool. Add confectioners' sugar and extract; beat until thick enough to spread easily. Spread over brownies.

Yield: about 2 dozen
(about 1½ cups icing)

*The original recipe called for coconut instead of chocolate chips.

132

Brandied Pecan-Fig Compote

In our culture, figs can be overlooked in favor of more widely produced fruit. While their season is short in most places, dried figs, like prunes, can be cooked into delicious dishes that add to our wintertime enjoyment. Dried figs pair well with pecans, especially when cooked with a splash of brandy. Of course, fresh figs contribute fabulously to a cheese plate.

If you loved Fig Newtons as a child, you will love this dessert. The grittiness of the seeds that stuck to your teeth all those years ago remains in this treat today. A friend, who at late middle age still sneaks a "Newton" now and again, says that in college she put whipped cream on them and ate them out of a dish with a spoon. When no one was looking, she'd eat the cookies out of hand, dipping them into the whipped cream. This recipe is for her.

3 packages (9 ounces *each*) dried Calimyrna *or* Mission figs
2 cups water
1 cup sugar
1 cup brandy *or* fruity wine
3 tablespoons grated fresh gingerroot
2 teaspoons lemon zest
½ cup chopped pecans, toasted
Whipped cream and additional toasted pecans

In a heavy saucepan, combine the figs, water, sugar, brandy or wine, ginger and lemon zest. Bring to a boil over medium heat, stirring constantly. Reduce heat to low; cover and simmer for about 1 hour or until figs are tender and most of the liquid is absorbed (do not overcook; mixture will thicken when processed). Cool.

Stir in pecans. Place a third of the mixture in a food processor; pulse 4-5 times or until compote becomes spreadable but not puréed. Repeat with remaining mixture in two batches. Compote may be made up to 3 days ahead and stored in the refrigerator. To serve, spoon into dessert dishes; top with a dollop of whipped cream and a sprinkle of toasted pecans.

Yield: about 3 cups

Variations: Make individual tartlets by serving the compote in 6 to 8 baked puff pastry shells; place a layer of toasted pecans in the shells before filling with compote.

For an appetizer or to accompany an entrée salad, wrap a small round of Brie—topped with toasted pecans and 2 tablespoons compote—in a sheet of puff pastry. Bake at 350° for 20 minutes or until pastry is golden brown.

133

Irresistible Baked Pears

Pears are underused at dessert time. Apples take over, and we forget there are other beckoning fruits available for after-dinner enjoyment. Although the choice of sauces "sweetens the pot," so to say, the simple baked pears are a treat unto themselves. Bartlett or Red Crimson varieties are preferred for this recipe, and make sure the pears aren't overly ripe.

4 large firm pears
¾ cup lemon *or* lime juice
¼ cup sugar, optional
¼ cup pecan pieces
Caramel Sauce
6 tablespoons butter (preferably unsalted)
½ cup packed brown sugar
1 cup heavy whipping cream
½ cup chopped pecans, toasted
1 teaspoon vanilla extract
Chocolate Sauce
1 cup heavy whipping cream
8 ounces bittersweet *or* semisweet chocolate,
   coarsely chopped
¼ cup sugar
½ cup chopped pecans, toasted
2 teaspoons vanilla extract

Peel, halve and core the pears; place in a large bowl. Add lemon or lime juice; toss gently to coat.

Arrange pears, cut side down, in a single layer in a greased shallow baking dish. Pour remaining juice from bowl over pears; add enough water to bring level up to about ¼ inch. Sprinkle sugar if desired and pecans over pears. Bake, uncovered, for 15 minutes or until tender (not mushy). Meanwhile, make the sauce of your choice.

For caramel sauce, melt butter and brown sugar in a heavy saucepan, stirring to prevent scorching. Cook for 3 minutes or until the sugar has melted and mixture is foamy. Slowly add cream, stirring or whisking to prevent mixture from boiling over.

Cook for 8–10 minutes, stirring occasionally, until sauce is thick and creamy. Add pecans and vanilla; stir to blend.

For chocolate sauce, place cream, chocolate and sugar in the top of a double boiler over medium heat. Cook until sauce is thick, stirring to prevent scorching. Add pecans and vanilla; stir to blend.

To serve, place one or two pear halves on each dessert plate; drizzle with warm caramel or chocolate sauce, or some of both. Pass remaining sauce.

Yield: 4-8 servings (about 1½ cups of each sauce)

Autumn Apple-Pecan Crisp with Bitters

On a crisp autumn day, what could be better than an apple crisp right out of the oven?

A crunchy apple just picked from the tree delights the taste buds, and a baked apple dessert teamed with all the right spices makes us enjoy putting on a sweater for extra coziness.

While the bitters gives a slightly distinctive flavor, the news in this recipe comes from the pairing of the pecans with the other ingredients. This dessert goes very well after a casual meal, such as a hearty soup. Leftover apple crisp is great for breakfast! Some unconventional people put it on top of oatmeal.

6 large tart apples
1 tablespoon angostura bitters
1 cup all-purpose flour
1 cup packed brown sugar
2 tablespoons rolled oats
1 teaspoon orange zest

1½ teaspoons ground cinnamon
½ teaspoon ground nutmeg
½ teaspoon ground cloves
¼ teaspoon salt
½ cup cold butter
½ cup finely chopped pecans
Whipped cream *or* vanilla *or* ginger ice cream

Preheat oven to 350°. Peel, core and slice the apples. Arrange in a greased 11-inch x 7-inch x 2-inch baking dish. Drizzle with bitters. In a mixing bowl, combine the flour, brown sugar, oats, orange zest, spices and salt; cut in butter until mixture is crumbly. Mix in pecans. Sprinkle over apples. Bake for 45 minutes or until apples are tender. Serve warm with whipped cream or ice cream.

Yield: 6-8 servings

136

In a Nutshell

Among some pecan fanciers, there is a debate as to whether a pecan tree is prettier in full leaf or etched against the horizon in winter bareness. It's a toss-up!

Gingered Pumpkin Cheesecake

No other dessert spells autumn or winter quite the way this one can when it appears on a buffet. The beautiful color alone would demand its presence at a game-day party or holiday celebration. Its richness is palpable, and one small piece is a sufficient serving size. Its mild sweetness causes even non-dessert eaters to return for another tiny portion. The pecans round out the punch that the cheesecake so smoothly packs.

If desired, sprinkle some extra toasted pecans over the cheesecake. Also, some hedonists will expect whipped topping—either on top or passed at the table.

2 cups gingersnap crumbs (about ½ pound of cookies)

⅓ cup butter (preferably unsalted), melted

½ cup coarsely chopped pecans, toasted

3 packages (8 ounces *each*) cream cheese, softened

½ cup sugar

½ cup packed light brown sugar

3 eggs, lightly beaten

1 can (15 ounces) unsweetened pumpkin purée

¼ cup sour cream

3 teaspoons vanilla extract

1½ teaspoons ground cinnamon

½ teaspoon ground nutmeg

½ teaspoon ground ginger

Preheat oven to 375°. In a bowl, combine the gingersnap crumbs and butter until well blended. Press crumb mixture firmly onto the bottom and about 1 inch up the sides of a greased 9- or 10-inch springform pan. Place on a baking sheet. Bake for 10 minutes or until crisp. Sprinkle pecans over crust. Set aside.

Reduce heat to 350°. For the filling, in a mixing bowl, beat cream cheese and sugars until smooth. Add eggs; beat on low speed just until combined. Add pumpkin, sour cream, vanilla and spices; beat until combined. Pour over crust.

Bake for 35–40 minutes or until center is almost set. Cool on a wire rack in a draft-free location for 10 minutes. Carefully run a knife around edge of pan to loosen; cool 1 hour longer. Cover and refrigerate overnight. Remove sides of pan before slicing cheesecake.

Yield: at least 12 servings

137

ODDMENTS
Condiments and Can't-Be-Categorized

Some recipes simply defy being categorized. When I found a few items that were well worth including, but didn't fit into the previous chapters, I decided to group them together. For example, the Canned Pecans recipe harkens back to an earlier era, while the Honey Pecan Butter recipe appears here but is mentioned throughout the book because of its utilitarian appeal.

Suffice it to say, the theme is purely the enjoyment of pecans ... as is my intended theme for this entire book. Thus I invite you to join my enjoyment of one of nature's most beneficial treats.

Who really needs to "can" pecans in today's world? The answer would be "no one." However, since we have traced the evolution of this important nut throughout its history, it would be remiss of me not to show how some home cooks have preserved the pecan for future use. Fortunately for us "moderns," cooking with pecans is enormously easier today.

With spreads, nut butters and compotes on hand, we can dress up the most basic of meals. With a little planning, we can turn to our refrigerators for a collection of pecan "oddments" that will enhance even—shall I say it—a dull, homely meal!

Canned Pecans

This recipe comes from "The Art of Southern Cooking," a cookbook published in Perry, Georgia, in 1967. The author, Mrs. Mildred Warren, compiled the recipes from those she'd written for a food column in the local newspaper.

With fresh pecans available through many sources nowadays, we do not need to go to great lengths to save our pecans to the extent we did in the past. However, the recipe indicates the degree to which pecans have been valued in our culture for many years.

Today, we don't need to can our seasonal food treasures; we just put them in a ziplock bag and throw them in the freezer. But remember that freezers have not always been available for storing pecans for months at a time, and old-fashioned refrigerators were too small to keep 10 or more pounds of pecans over long periods.

In warm climates, rancidity can ruin a prized stash of picked-out pecans. As strange as "canning" pecans might sound from today's vantage point, that method has saved many a cook when it came time to do holiday cooking!

Mrs. Warren reminds us that the oven does all the work in this process. At the time, it must have been a good feeling to look in the pantry and see 8 cups of preserved pecans waiting to be used. I get the same feeling from looking in my freezer!

4 pint-size screw-top jars
8 cups raw shelled pecans (preferably halves)

Fill each jar with 2 cups of pecans, leaving enough room at the top to crumple a small piece of brown paper (part of a grocery bag will do) to stuff on top of the pecans. Screw tops on jars tightly. Set jars in a cold oven and turn heat to 250°. After oven is preheated, bake pecans for 45 minutes. Turn oven off and leave jars in oven until cool.

139

Yield: 4 pints

Pecan Butter to Spread on Nearly Everything

When snacking on an apple, increase its hunger-satisfying properties by spreading 1 teaspoon of this pecan butter over the slices. The spread isn't bad with jelly either. Given the nutrition in even a small amount of pecans, our diets profit from the protein they contain.

1 cup pecan pieces
2 tablespoons pecan oil *or* melted butter
1 to 1½ teaspoons fresh lemon juice
1 teaspoon Worcestershire sauce, optional
½ teaspoon salt

Preheat oven to 350°. In a bowl, toss all ingredients until pecans are coated. Place pecans in a single layer on an ungreased baking sheet. Bake for 10 minutes. Cool. Transfer pecans to a food processor; pulse until mixture is smooth and spreadable.

Yield: about 1 cup

140

Honey Pecan Butter

Spreads like this can be bought at some expense from various pecan outlets. Why not make your own and choose the flavor of honey you most prefer? It's quick and easy, tastes homemade and keeps well in the refrigerator. Serve on toast, bread, waffles and pancakes ... or eat it with a spoon for the simplest of snacks. In decorative jars, this butter would make a great gift!

1 cup butter, softened
¼ cup honey
½ cup pecan pieces, toasted if desired

In a small mixing bowl, beat the butter and honey until well blended. Add pecans and mix until evenly distributed. Store in airtight jars in the refrigerator.

Yield: about 1¾ cups

Party-Time Pecan Butter Spread

Good on crackers or toasted pumpernickel triangles, this rich spread would nicely accompany an entrée salad. It also pairs well with the Brandied Pecan-Fig Compote (recipe on page 133). The flavor is not unlike that of baked Brie, and its preparation can be done in less time.

¼ cup pecan pieces
2 tablespoons pecan oil *or* peanut oil
8 ounces Brie cheese, rind removed and cubed
1 package (3 ounces) cream cheese, cubed
2 tablespoons sherry
¼ teaspoon salt
Additional roasted pecans, optional

Place pecans and oil in a food processor; pulse until combined. Add the cheeses, sherry and salt; pulse until creamy. Transfer to a serving bowl; sprinkle with roasted pecans if desired. Store in the refrigerator.

Yield: about 1½ cups

Variation: Add 1 tablespoon of Cambozola, Gorgonzola or other blue cheese for a slightly stronger flavor.

141

Spiced Sweet Potato Butter

This variation is sometimes offered in vegetarian restaurants as a replacement for dairy butter. Spread on bread or crackers or use as a dip with celery sticks.

1 medium onion
2 medium sweet potatoes *or* yams
2 teaspoons pecan oil *or* olive oil
3 tablespoons pecan pieces, toasted *or* roasted
   or Candied Gingered Pecans (recipe on
   page 28)
1 tablespoon lavender honey, optional
1 teaspoon ground cinnamon
½ teaspoon ground cloves
½ teaspoon ground ginger

142

Preheat oven to 400°. Remove outermost layer of onion, leaving inner skin. Coat the onion and sweet potatoes with oil. Wrap individually in foil; bake for 1 hour or until soft.

Remove foil. When cool enough to handle, peel tough outer layer of onion and chop into six pieces and peel the sweet potatoes.

In a food processor, grind pecans to a fine meal. Add onion, sweet potatoes, honey if desired, cinnamon, cloves and ginger; process until puréed. Transfer to a bowl. Serve warm or at room temperature. Store in the refrigerator for up to 3 days.

Yield: about 1½ cups

Lemony Pecan Mayonnaise

Many good cooks fear homemade mayonnaise. No need to be afraid, for there's always the good store-bought kind if your attempt to make it fails. However, there's nothing better with a beautifully ripe tomato or crisp spears of blanched baby okra or on a BLT on a hot summer's day.

With pecans added, this mayonnaise becomes a special treat in a Waldorf or chicken salad. The list of reasons to make it fresh and use it often goes on and on.

It is nearly impossible to make homemade mayonnaise without a raw egg, so if its presence bothers you, it's best to skip it and just listen to other people's raves. For best results, make sure all ingredients are at room temperature. And if you use a hand blender, all ingredients can be combined simultaneously.

1 egg
1 tablespoon lemon juice
½ teaspoon salt
½ teaspoon white pepper
½ teaspoon dry mustard, optional
1 cup pecan oil *or* ½ cup extra virgin olive oil
   and ½ cup light olive oil
¼ cup pecan pieces

In a blender, combine the egg, lemon juice, salt, pepper and mustard if desired; pulse until well combined. While blender is running, slowly add oil in a steady stream through the hole in the lid. As the mixture absorbs the oil, an emulsion will be achieved, and the mixture will suddenly resemble mayonnaise. Add pecans at the last pulsing, just to incorporate. Refrigerate until using; best to use the day it's made.

143

Yield: about 1 cup

In a Nutshell

Can you imagine a pecan skyscraper? It would take 11,624 pecans, stacked end to end, to reach the top of the Empire State Building.

—*North Carolina Pecan Growers Association*

Something-Different Pecan Pesto

Pesto enhances so many Italian dishes that it's helpful to have more than one way to make it. Pine nuts are typically used in pesto, as are walnuts; when you try it with pecans, you will return to that method time and time again. The result is a brand-new flavor to use with your favorite pasta. Feel free to add more garlic if you prefer.

1½ cups tightly packed fresh basil leaves
¾ cup pecan oil *or* olive oil
¾ cup pecan pieces
1 clove garlic
1 teaspoon salt
1 teaspoon black pepper

Place basil and oil in a blender or food processor; pulse until basil is finely chopped. Add the remaining ingredients; pulse until pecans are ground and mixture is well combined. Store in the refrigerator. Pesto keeps about 1 week without losing flavor; it can also be frozen without loss of flavor.

Yield: about 1½ cups

144

Surprise Hummus

This hummus features the usual garbanzo beans and seasonings, but the surprise is pecans, which add a whole new dimension. Serve as a dip with toasted pita triangles and raw vegetables.

1 cup pecan oil *or* olive oil, *divided*
½ cup pecan pieces
1½ cups canned garbanzo beans
1 to 2 cloves garlic
2 tablespoons fresh lemon *or* lime juice
1 teaspoon salt
1 teaspoon black pepper

In a food processor, combine ½ cup oil and pecans; pulse until a paste is formed. Add the beans, garlic, lemon or lime juice, salt, pepper and remaining oil; pulse until all ingredients are well combined. Test for seasoning and adjust if needed. Transfer to a serving bowl. Refrigerate leftovers.

Yield: about 2½ cups

Jalapeño Cranberry Compote

Most ready-made compotes of this type have pectin added to make the mixture "jell." I prefer this homemade version, which jells from a slow cooking time, the natural sugar in the fruit and the relatively small amount of added sugar.

A compote differs from a chutney in that it doesn't include onions or celery. Normally, it is closer to a conserve—a cooked fruit mixture. Not intended to be jelly or chutney, this compote goes with an entrée, rather than at breakfast as a sweet. Serve with roasted meats, as an accompaniment to casseroles on a buffet or on a cheese plate along with crackers or toast points. Try it on a turkey sandwich made with crusty sourdough bread ... you'll want more!

1 small Mandarin *or* satsuma orange *or*
   2 clementines
2 packages (12 ounces *each*) fresh *or* frozen
   cranberries
1 cup sugar
2 teaspoons canned sliced jalapeño peppers
1 tablespoon ground cinnamon
1 teaspoon ground cloves
½ cup pecan pieces, toasted

Pulse the orange (including rind) in a food processor until coarsely chopped. Place in a 2-quart saucepan. Add the cranberries, sugar, jalapeños, cinnamon and cloves. Cover and cook over low heat for 2-4 hours or until thickened, stirring every 30 minutes and checking occasionally to make sure the mixture doesn't boil over.

(If your cooking time gets interrupted, no harm is done. Turn off the heat and let the compote rest. Start cooking again and continue, over low heat, stirring occasionally to be sure mixture doesn't stick to the bottom of the pan.)

Cool; stir in pecans. Store in jars or airtight containers in the refrigerator.

Yield: about 4½ cups

145

In a Nutshell

To fill an Olympic-size swimming pool, you'd need 144 million pecans.
—*North Carolina Pecan Growers Association*

Toasted Granola

Granola belongs in most pantries. Nutritious, satisfying and convenient, it can be nibbled from a plastic bag while hiking, and it is a welcome addition to cereal and yogurt. Check your local health food store for dried unsweetened coconut flakes—they're good in this recipe.

6 cups rolled oats

1¾ cups chopped pecans

1⅓ cups flaked coconut

1 cup wheat germ

¾ cup honey

¼ cup water

½ cup pecan oil *or* peanut oil

3 teaspoons vanilla extract

1 teaspoon ground cinnamon

1 teaspoon ground nutmeg

½ teaspoon ground cloves

½ teaspoon salt

Preheat oven to 250°. In a large bowl, combine the oats, pecans, coconut and wheat germ; set aside. In a small saucepan, heat the honey and water, stirring frequently, until mixture is thoroughly heated and begins to thin. Remove from the heat; stir in oil and vanilla.

Pour over oat mixture and mix well. Add spices and salt, stirring to blend. Pour into two greased 13-inch x 9-inch x 2-inch baking pans. Bake for 1 hour, stirring every 15 minutes. Cool. Store in an airtight container.

Yield: 10 cups

Variation: Add raisins and chopped dried apricots to make your own GORP (see GOCP recipe on page 27).

In a Nutshell

Of all tree nuts, pecans suffer most in the supermarket. With a dried and shriveled appearance, they do not beckon buyers. Order directly from a respected vendor and get a fresh, plump product with a full, rich flavor.

146

Chocolate Bark with Lots of Bite

This novelty recipe would make a good gift or party item. For a teen party, omit the cayenne, chili powder and cherries, and add M&M's or Butterfinger Bits.

4 cups pecan halves (1 pound)
2 tablespoons butter, melted
1 tablespoon sugar
1 teaspoon salt
½ teaspoon ground cinnamon
½ teaspoon cayenne pepper, optional
½ teaspoon chili powder, optional
1 package (12 ounces) semisweet chocolate chips
4½ tablespoons vegetable oil, *divided*
1 package (11½ ounces) milk chocolate chips
1 package (10 to 12 ounces) vanilla *or* white chips
½ to ¾ cup dried cherries, optional

Preheat oven to 325°. Place the pecans in a bowl; add butter and toss. Combine the sugar, salt, cinnamon, and cayenne and chili powder if desired; sprinkle over pecans and toss to coat. Spread in a single layer on a baking sheet. Bake for 25 minutes or until golden brown. Cool (leaving pecans on the pan).

In a microwave-safe bowl, combine the semisweet chips and 1½ tablespoons oil; microwave at 50% power for 1 minute; stir. Microwave 1 minute longer or as needed, stirring after each minute, until chips are melted and mixture is pourable (be careful not to overheat). Stir until chocolate is smooth, then immediately drizzle over pecans, distributing evenly and making a pattern over the nuts' surface.

Repeat the process with the milk chocolate and vanilla chips, melting each package with 1½ tablespoons oil. When drizzling over the pecans, make sure all colors of chocolate are visible. Sprinkle with cherries if desired. Let stand until set. Break into serving-size pieces. Store in an airtight container.

147

Yield: about 3 pounds

Variation: Make a dessert pizza by arranging the pecans in a large circle and pouring the melted chocolate in a circular motion. On top, arrange a variety of soft candies to imitate pizza slices. This confection is tricky to cut and keep the pieces intact (using a pizza cutter just before the chocolate hardens is worth a try). But if they break, no one will care, as everyone will love eating it.

HOW TO SPEAK "PECAN"

Although almost no one has trouble saying "walnut" with confidence, some people shy away from the pronunciation of "pecan." Is it PEE-kan, pih-KAHN or even PECK-an, they wonder.

Their consternation is justified, as the word has been pronounced and mispronounced all over the country. Seemingly there is no fixed way to say "pecan," as it has fallen victim to regional differences. Different pecan-growing areas take their pick of the above pronunciations, and very little changes the belief of any particular area.

I know of two men who have worked side by side in a commercial orchard for years, and to hear each of them say pecan is to hear two of the above accents. While they do not seem to argue about the way to say the word, neither man changes his own take on it from year to year.

Natives of the various pecan-growing areas do not much care what the dictionary says; more important to them is how their grandparents said pecan. The "PEE-kan" people ignore the "pih-KAHN" crowd and vice versa.

In essence, the way to say pecan depends on where you are. I'm a pih-KAHN person myself, to tell the truth, but you can say what makes you happy.

On the other hand, I feel strongly about the pronunciation of "praline." That's another story! To me, it's PRAH-leen, and I have to admit that PRAY-leen grates on me. Now that I think about it, the pecan industry should adopt a slogan that says, "If you like pih-KAHNS, you'll love PRAH-leens!" That wording would both bring clarity and please me enormously.

Now for Some Insiders' Terminology

Unless you've grown up in the pecan business—whether growing, shelling or selling them—you probably know only how to eat the nuts or cook with them. To fully appreciate pecans, it is imperative that the eager consumer know as much as possible about them.

Wine connoisseurs study the grape and learn all they can about viticulture—the soil, the climate and the general conditions optimal for the production of the best possible vintage. Likewise, we want to study the pecan—its varieties, its growing conditions and the terms

149

used by those who are involved with the pecan on a daily basis.

Commercial orchards spend much of the fall engaged in reaping what they have been sowing for many months. All the fastidious treatment will begin to pay off, but much care has to be taken not to damage the trees or the nuts when work begins. "Gently but firmly" is the motto.

Harvesting machinery is expensive, and crews are hired to get the crop to the marketplace. At large orchards, crew members often live on the premises during harvesttime, returning to their hometowns or native countries afterward, unless they stay on to help bring in peaches or other seasonal crops.

150

As in any industry, there is a vocabulary used by the insiders. At a commercial orchard or shelling plant, you might hear some of the following colorful terms:

Grape-like cluster—a term used to describe the appearance and configuration of pecans growing on a branch (see the photo on page 12). Visiting a pecan grower in Texas, cereal magnate C.W. Post commented that the nuts grew in beautiful "grape-like clusters." He was so impressed that he went home and named his new cereal "Grape-Nuts."

Stick tights—nuts whose hull sticks to the outer shell so they cannot fall off the tree onto the ground. This situation calls for an additional step to free the recalcitrant nuts for use.

Shake tree—to rid the trees of their nuts by means of a shaker machine, which literally grasps the trunk with a tong-like device that shakes the entire tree. Nuts rain down as if caught in a storm. Seen at a distance, the "tongs" resemble those used by a chef.

Bump tree—to bump the tree (with the machine) after the first shake to loosen only nuts that are ready to fall

Slip bark—when the machine's tongs grasp the tree too tightly and damage the bark

Windrow—the "alley" between the rows of trees. Once the nuts have fallen to the ground, a machine sweeps them out from under the trees and into neat rows so another machine can "vacuum" them into a wagon.

"Hoover"—the machine that "vacuums" the pecans from the windrows into the wagon (see the photo on page 152)

Dump—the volume of harvested product contained in the dump wagon before it's sorted

Pounds/Dump—the number of pounds of pecans contained in the total dump, vis-à-vis debris such as limbs or branches

Wet vs. Dry—the percentage of moisture in the pecan kernel, which indicates the ripeness of the nutmeat. Suitable moisture is 6–7%; thus, a moisture level of 10–20% indicates greenness.

Green wet—an immature kernel that's not yet ripe

Water wet—moisture from rain, not from greenness

De-hull—the process used to free the nut from its hull

Pop—a nut that has little or no meat inside the shell

Filled out—a nut with a high percentage of meat inside the shell

Wafer or "light"—a nut whose kernel did not fill out completely and is very light in weight

Paper shells—varieties of pecans that have a thinner shell than other types. The Schley pecan is one variety that has been bred to have a thinner shell, which makes the shelling process easier.

B-Grade—a classification for nuts that are of inferior grade but still have value. The superior grades are often sold as halves in gift baskets, whereas B-Grades are sold to the confectionery industry for baking and candymaking.

Count—the number of pecans in a 1-pound sample

Yield—the percentage of nutmeat to total weight of in-shell nut

151

PECANS
Past and Present

Past ...

Speakers of English call them "pecans" ... Native Americans referred to them as "pacanes" ... Spanish explorers in the 16th century came to call them "pacanos" ... while the French colonists around New Orleans designated them as "pecanes" in the early 18th century.

Basically, the Native Americans got it right—"pacane" is the Algonquin word for "nut too hard to be cracked by hand." Some sources state the term to similarly mean "nut that must be cracked with a stone."

Whatever the exact phrasing, the image is explicit: Early residents of the lower part of the North American continent amassing sustenance in a hard world by sitting around the fire, cracking nuts with a stone. Eight or nine thousand years ago, in the early Archaic period, the pacane came in very handy.

Immediate gratification may have been involved—those cracking the nuts could have eaten in one sitting all the nutmeat they extracted. More likely, their efforts were toward storage of the food for later sustenance. In winter, after the meat source had dwindled or expired, the residents turned to their stores, sequestered in the trunks of trees or otherwise hidden.

The earliest indication of pecan use on this continent goes back to archaeological evidence found as far north as present-day Illinois, dating from 9,000 years ago. Leaf and seed remains indicate the presence of hickory nuts as a natural food source (pecans belong to the hickory family). This is how the pecan received its botanical name, *Carya illinoinensis,* in 1969.

During the 16th century and doubtless much earlier, Native Americans of the southern part of what is now the United States had come to rely on pecans in their diets. In some native cultures, February was called "the nut moon," as by then other sources of food had been consumed, thus leaving the inhabitants to rely on nuts they had stored.

Native migration patterns indicate tribal movement from northern Mexico into the U.S., tracing the pecan season along river bottoms and other fertile areas. Even in areas where meat and fish were abundantly available, pecans rounded out the native diet for centuries.

153

The Very Versatile Nut

The Indians who lived in pecan country devised uses for the tree's produce beyond that of food source. Hickory wood, especially pacane wood, widely used by the Ojibwa tribe, proved suitable for making bows and finishing off baskets.

Other native tribes extracted paste and oil from the pecan to devise medicinal remedies, preceding the modern use of castor oil as a palliative. These remedies helped abate a long list of ills, not the least of which were constipation and intestinal worms. Additionally, skin eruptions, gynecological problems, gastrointestinal upsets, rheumatism, colds and liver dysfunction appeared to respond to the use of pecans and their derivatives.

One early European observer, apparently having followed Indian instructions, wrote, "It's commended for a good Remedy in Dolors, and Gripes of the Belly; whilst new it has a pleasant Taste; but after six Months, it decays and grows acid." (Ash, 1682)

On a lighter note, pecans even filled the void when Native Americans sought a mood-brightening beverage. Through a process of boiling and fermentation, they created a potion called "powcohicoria," which became popular wherever pecans thrived.

When the Spanish Conquistadors hit the southern shores of North America, having come up from the Caribbean Islands, the pecan was among the first foods they were introduced to. The nut was flavorful and abundant, and natives helped the visitors adapt them for everyday use.

Hernando de Soto was one of the first European explorers to develop a taste for pecans, writing favorably of them in his journals between 1539 and 1542. Finding large supplies of both the nuts and their oil among the Indians, he copied their techniques of preparation and bartered with them to obtain nuts for his own use. Thus, pecans became a medium of exchange.

Explorer Waxes Eloquent

Of all the Europeans who came to our shores, a Spaniard named Alvar Nunez wrote the most eloquently and extensively of pecans. Known in history by his descriptive nickname "Cabeza de Vaca" (Cowhead), the explorer was shipwrecked off Galveston in 1528 and captured by the Karankawa tribe. He spent seven years subsisting intermittently on pecans. When other food supplies had dried up, he and his captors were left to forage among the wild trees for nuts.

In his diary, Cabeza de Vaca wrote about being tied to a tree and having nothing to eat but

pound after pound of "nueces." Another word for pecans, nueces is used today both in Mexico and parts of Texas, where there is a Nueces River—an appropriate name since pecans thrive in fertile river bottoms.

Cabeza de Vaca observed one of the Indians' religious rituals of eating only nueces for two months, which was apparently a gesture of gratitude to their deity. He also noted the Indians' large harvest of pecans in preparation for the following year, when the crop would be much sparser, reflecting the inborn trait of the pecan tree to be an "alternate bearer"—a tree that produces a big crop every other year.

Maintaining a full supply was imperative, as the rich nuts provided essential health benefits. In other diaries, observers noted that when migrating or going off in search of meat or game, the Indians would take large supplies of roasted nueces to guarantee nourishment on the trip.

Having used nueces for centuries, the Mexicans developed wide production throughout the northern reaches of their country. By the 17th century, documentation indicates that the pecan had attained commercial value in Mexico due to its usefulness and popularity.

Interestingly, when Cabeza de Vaca returned home to Spain, instead of telling bitter stories of his captivity, he regaled the Queen of Spain

with tales of his adventures. He also presented her with a gift of pecans, thus successfully introducing our native nut to Europe at the royal level.

155

We can thank the historic Native American population for the role pecans play in our modern everyday life. They introduced the European arrivals in Texas, Georgia, Florida and other parts of the South to the nutritious, essential nut. Then they were generous in teaching the Colonists to maximize their use of this natural resource. Their subsistence, and at times that of our ancestors, depended on the availability of pecans for food.

The French were next to be introduced to this new food source. Settling in Louisiana, they'd brought their own recipes and favored ingredients, which lasted for a time. They learned from the Choctaw, Cherokee and other native tribes how to incorporate pecans into their developing Creole cuisine.

Living in New Orleans between 1718 and 1734, Le Page du Pratz wrote in his *Histoire de la Louisiane* that pecans had "a flavor so fine that the French make 'pralines' of them as good as those made of almonds."

After a time, the French settlers fully embraced the native pecan and added them to their diet. Soon they preferred the special flavor of pecans to the nuts they had known in their homeland.

Promoted by Presidents

Later in that same century, as the United States began to take shape as an entity separate from England, at least two of the new country's leaders knew about and promoted pecans. After a trip to the Mississippi Valley in 1775, Thomas Jefferson excitedly brought back to Virginia the nuts and seedlings to share with George Washington. Curious farmers, both of the future presidents delighted in the propagation of a new, tasty crop.

Although Jefferson may not have developed recipes for his favorite nut, records indicate that he enjoyed snacking on his "Mississippi Nuts," as he called them.

Oddly, there is scientific evidence of the presence of pecans in northern areas to which they were not native and couldn't have survived. In North and South Dakota, the Dakota tribes had words for these nuts and clearly were familiar with them. Scientists debate the question of whether the northern tribes migrated south to acquire pecans as a foodstuff, or whether the southern tribes traveled north in search of meat. Regardless, there is no question that pecans were an object of trade and commerce, among the Indians and then the Colonists.

In 1792, noted botanist William Bartram wrote this about pecans: "The Creeks store up the last in their towns. I have seen above an (sic) hundred bushels of these nuts belonging to one family. They pound them to pieces, and then cast them into boiling water, which, after passing through fine strainers, preserves the most oily part of the liquid; this they call by a name which signifies hickory milk; it is as sweet and rich as fresh cream, and is an ingredient in most of their cookery, especially homony (sic) and corn cakes."

As time went on, Southern states, where pecans thrived, invested their time and energy in developing large stands of pecan trees. First, there were large groves of uncultivated or wild pecans; then orchards—intentional stands of planted trees—dotted the countryside. As farmers began to realize the commercial value, plus the culinary importance of pecans, they actually came to revere the nut.

Gardener Succeeds in Grafting

Until 1847, all pecans derived from native varieties. Even though attempts at grafting had been made, none had been successful. It took a slave gardener, remembered only by his first name of "Antoine," to create a "cultivar"—a cross between two different varieties of natives. This feat occurred on Oak Alley Plantation, between New Orleans and Baton Rouge, Louisiana.

The owner of nearby Anita Plantation had made several frustrated attempts at grafting, complaining of his failure to the owner of Oak Alley. Aware of the scientific work going on in his presence, Antoine continued his own efforts. When he succeeded, it isn't known whether Antoine was immediately compensated for his discovery; however, satisfaction alone must have been precious to him.

At the Philadelphia Centennial Exposition in 1876, some lasting recognition was awarded Antoine: His pecan variety was named "Best of Show" and named the "Centennial." Many of our best pecan strains have descended from that first cultivar.

New cultivars thrived at Oak Alley for several decades. As times changed, the "Antoine trees" were cut down to make more room to plant sugarcane. Although none of these original trees is known to exist today, records show where they once stood. At George Washington's Mount Vernon, there is one suspected "relative" of the early pecan trees, but only the suspicion is certain. Some records claim that three of the original "George Washington" trees survive at his Virginia home.

As pecan growers subsequently developed new varieties with thinner, easier-to-crack shells, and the technology to process the nuts, pecans acquired a high market value. The French settlers were the first to export them, sending them directly to the West Indies.

From the port at New Orleans, the ease of shipping large quantities of the valued nuts up the Mississippi or out to foreign users enhanced pecans' worth as a money crop. This trend took root in the 18th century and continued into the 19th.

As late as the end of the 19th century, Native Americans were still involved in facilitating pecan use. In San Antonio, Texas, Gustav Duerler started a pecan candy business. As his sales escalated, he found a pecan shortage, caused by a lack of growers and a limited commercial supply, so he turned to the Indians.

157

Eager for the money, the local tribesmen entered into a contract with the businessman. Soon, the pecans came to Mr. Duerler, wrapped in deerskins, still in the shell. Once the candymaker acquired his supply, he realized he was still in need of pickers.

Lacking machinery, he equipped willing laborers with a railroad spike to crack the nuts and a sack needle to extract the meat from the shell. Seemingly primitive by today's standards, the "technology" available at the time proved effective. It wasn't long before fully developed machinery came along, and growers began to thrive.

Present ...

Today, pecans rank No. 2 in the United States' nut production, just behind the peanut. Despite the fact that the peanut is not actually a nut, but a legume, pecans still rank second.

Unlike the walnut, which is basically a one-state product, grown principally in California, the pecan is a multi-state commodity. In the past, pecans grew in a band of states across the American South. While that may be true today to a certain extent, states like New Mexico, Kansas, Arizona and California—thanks to irrigation—can be contenders in the industry. In recent years, New Mexico has even challenged Texas in pecan production.

Basically, pecans still like river bottoms and fertile alluvial soil, which they find in Texas, Georgia, Louisiana, Mississippi, Florida and Alabama. They still prefer a relatively mild, wet climate, but they can grow, with encouragement, in other varied situations.

While Georgia usually leads the country in the production of "improved" pecan varieties, meaning grafted versions, Texas has normally been the leader in "native" types, which means that "wild" trees naturally predominate there.

There are proponents of both types of nuts, some who insist the best flavor can be found in natives, whereas other fans cling to the notion that an "improved" nut carries the day. Today, as a matter of practicality, the producing states try for the largest and best crop possible, regardless of the type of nut brought to fruition.

According to lore, "You cannot fool a pecan tree." While many plants and trees are damaged by coming forward too early in the spring and getting nipped by frost, once pecan trees have begun to bud, there is no more threat of a killing frost for that year. That belief holds true most years. Nature, with its vagaries, is not as smart as the *Carya illinoinensis*.

In wetter climates, irrigation is not a dire necessity; however, more plant diseases predominate. Conversely, the drier states save money by not fighting pests, yet they spend heavily on irrigation. Wherever the location, the pecan grower, like other farmers, must combat nature in some aspects of his business.

Pecans Need Publicity

Because pecans grow in so many states, organizing growers has proved fairly ineffective. Whereas California, the principal walnut producer, invests large sums of money in its promotion of its walnuts, pecan-producing states lag behind.

If consumption could be based on desirability, the pecan would doubtless lead the country in nut consumption. In a way, it's miraculous that the pecan is as well integrated into our food spending as it is, given its lack of publicity.

When taken into consideration the money that is spent promoting raisins, for example, it becomes clear that, with a portion of that advertising budget, pecans would move into the forefront of global use. While raisins are fairly nutritious, pecans are way out front in most nutritive elements, adding almost no sugar to the diet.

Advanced technology brings us ready-to-use pecans, shelled, in halves or in pieces. Although pecans are harvested in the fall, they are available during all seasons. Often they are dried briefly before packaging and are best kept refrigerated or frozen. Pecans can be

taken directly from the freezer and used immediately.

159

Often, pecans sit unnoticed until holiday cooking begins. When a cook thinks of autumn and winter desserts, she often remembers pecan pie and buys some aging pecans off the grocery store shelf. With this use, pecans do not get a fair chance at full entry into our everyday cuisine. They should appear on our table day in, day out, throughout the year.

We've forgotten what we learned from the early Native Americans, who were fully aware of the value of pecans and taught Colonists how to use them. They realized the nutritive and healing values of the pecan. They used them in favor of other food sources, seeing that much good came from them. They also caught on to the fact that the nuts worked well in trade, using them as a medium of exchange.

Now, when the United States needs more natural exports—as opposed to manufactured goods—the pecan is available. Being at its peak of nutritional value in the raw state, it could work well in a global market as an export item. Of course, convincing foreign markets of the pecan's usefulness might be difficult, since almost no marketing is done.

In our oversight, other countries like Australia, China and Israel are now producing their own pecan supply. In time, they can likely develop the pecan as a powerful export possibility, leaving us to wish we had beaten them to the idea!

160

Over 500 Varieties Exist

While some pecans still come from the old, original native trees, the "wild pecans" do not proliferate commercially as do the cultivars, numbering now over 500 varieties. In the Southwest, Indian names are often applied to emerging varieties, thus honoring the Native Americans who first brought our native pecan to our attention. We find varieties like "Pawnee," "Creek," "Apache" and "Cherokee" on the list of recent cultivars.

In other areas, such as in Georgia, the large "Desirable" is popular and is attractive in gift boxes. The "Stuart" is also popular, as is the smaller "Elliott." The "Schley" commands attention for its adaptability in various settings.

Regardless of how far these "improved" varieties have come, we still have Antoine to thank for his original "Centennial" breakthrough. We might rightfully call our modern nuts "Antoine's Gift." He is really the father of the pecans we know today.

Another name that could justifiably be applied is the "Native American Nut"—not only because of the fact that pecans come to us through the agriculture and resourcefulness of countless native tribes, but because the pecan is the only nut that is truly native to the United States. Other nuts thrive here because of the country's varied climate zones, but all of those were originally imported. Only the pecan started out here. So let's use the pecan—with gratitude and pride.

HOW DO PECANS LOVE YOU?

Let Us Count the Ways
(With Apologies to Elizabeth Barrett Browning)

A large part of this book revolves around my passion for pecans. As it turns out, the more important aspect of our involvement should originate in the pecans' love for us. They benefit us in many ways. Let us return to the Indians' regard for the pecan and discover how it can take care of us.

One Texas tribe even thought of the pecan as a deity. Medically speaking, they were right on point; vis-à-vis our health, the nut verges on being all-powerful.

For years, olives and olive oil have appeared on healthy diet lists. We are told to adhere to the Mediterranean Diet to ensure good health. Olives are known to be full of fat, but few people avoid them because of their caloric content. We eat olives because we know they are good for us.

Thanks to poor or no promotion, pecans quietly provide the same if not more health benefits than olives, yet their praises do not get sung. Like humble donors compared to blatant givers (every town has both types of philanthropists), pecans keep on giving without notice.

Someone with health concerns would incorporate pecans and their oil into his diet on a daily basis, finding ways to eliminate useless calories and enjoying those beneficial ones provided by pecans. "Calories" is not a dirty word; it is the qualifier "empty" that is our enemy. Any calorie provided by pecans will add value toward our well-being if added in reasonable amounts.

Pecans should figure into our diets in a preventive way, rather than as a treatment. Although Native Americans used them medicinally, we have the opportunity to embrace the nuts in order to stay healthy rather than to cure us.

So far, to my knowledge, there has never been a Pecan Diet, but there should be one. Such a regimen would include reasonably sized portions, high fiber content, consumption of beneficial oils and a dearth of empty calories. Many dishes included in this book would fit nicely into this diet.

The Southern Diet might be an appropriate name for this regimen; however, that terminology evokes notions of yeast rolls, hot biscuits and other fattening treats. Perhaps the Pecan Belt Diet would be better, engendering the idea of tightening our belts (denoting a diminishing waist size) as we maintain our weight the healthy, sensible way!

Here are some facts that support the creation of a Pecan Diet.

Pecans ...

- are low in sodium, thus they add nutrition without adding salt to low-sodium diets.

- are high in fiber, thus they add bulk while providing nutrition.

- furnish calcium, phosphorous, iron, potassium and magnesium to our diets.

- are 73.41% fat, so they are a substantial source of energy. Twenty pecan halves provide about 100 calories filled with long-lasting benefits, as compared to foods with the same caloric content and fewer or no health benefits.

- are a good source of the B vitamins thiamin, riboflavin and niacin.

- are made up of 10.43% protein, which puts them on good-diet lists.

- have been proven to contribute toward reducing incidences of degenerative and chronic diseases, such as Alzheimer's and Parkinson's, and even some types of cancer.

- benefit us through their high levels of mono-unsaturated fatty acids (oleic—the same fatty acid in olives—and linoleic) that combat the "bad" fats we consume in the rest of our diet.

- ranked highest in a test of the antioxidant capacity of over 100 foods. The test drew attention to the nut group, and pecans ranked higher than any other nut for their ability to minimize cell damage brought on by the aging process.

- add magnesium, copper and manganese to our diets, all valuable to the intake of a healthy person.

- have been shown to reduce the "bad" LDL in our cholesterol levels by 6%, as detected by a study at New Mexico University.

- have been shown, in some cases, to reduce cholesterol levels as much as medication directed toward that purpose. For every 1% of LDL reduction, there is a 1.5% reduction in incidence of coronary heart disease. Thus, a pecan diet in the Loma Linda and Texas A&M studies would correspond to a 25% decreased risk of heart disease.

- have been shown to not only contribute toward lowering the "bad" LDL in our cholesterol levels, but also to raise the "good" HDL levels.

- naturally contain plant sterols in the form of beta-sitosterol in concentrated amounts, a component that affects the absorption of cholesterol in our bodies.

- have been shown to lower triglycerides in the blood, an occurrence similar in benefit to lowering cholesterol in the blood.

- contain phytochemicals that offer antioxidant protection from diseases other than heart disease and cancer—diabetes, for instance. Some studies indicate that pecans in a diet can help reduce blood sugar levels, which should be of great interest to diabetics.

- are high in zinc, a mineral that helps the body generate testosterone. Both men and women benefit from good levels of testosterone, as it affects sexual desire in a positive way.

- contain an essential oil that can be used as an inhalant as well as a healing topical oil. Putting a few drops of the oil on a cloth and breathing it in stimulates the body to make antibodies, endorphins and neurotrans-mitters that help strengthen the body's immune system.

- contain good levels of vitamin E, one advantage being that their alpha tocopherol level as part of vitamin E is high. This presence is helpful in smoothing out arterial lining, thus reducing the collection of blood platelets that can cause blockage in the arteries.

165

Pecans cannot do it alone. We must incorporate them into our diets along with many other wholesome foods such as fresh vegetables, grains and fruits. Although Native Americans sometimes referred to the pecan tree as "Great Spirit," we must thank the pecan and adopt a healthy approach to eating, partaking daily of its many benefits. We are in charge of our own health; we must love ourselves as pecans love us, in all of these ways and more.

AFTERWORD

Every pecan-growing state can find a fact that brings with it a boast. Most years, Georgia outproduces other states in growing certain varieties. Texas is home to the most native varieties, whereas New Mexico is gaining on both states in number of pounds produced.

Where does that leave Louisiana, my home state? For one thing, it grows a lot of the small, sweet "natives" or "seedlings."

Some enthusiasts, even one from Georgia like William S. Morris III, commented upon receiving a gift of Louisiana pecans, "I think the seedling pecans are the best of all. While we have made great strides in creating improved and larger varieties of pecans, there is nothing like the flavor of the seedling. It packs a lot of flavor in such a small package."

Even though that statement constitutes praise from a high place, Louisiana has exclusive bragging rights to another fact: It can claim the renowned writer Ernest Gaines as one of its citizens. After wandering far and wide, Mr. Gaines returned to his home state to realize himself as a writer.

In an autobiographical essay he wrote for *The Southern Review,* published at Louisiana State University, Mr. Gaines remembers spending a lot of time on a plantation in South Louisiana where his grandmother worked. Like many of us as we reflect on chores thrust upon us as children, he tells of being assigned the job of picking up pecans in the yard.

While this task was probably not fun—perhaps in the same category with picking out pecans for adult candymakers—Mr. Gaines surely was given an easier job. Try picking the meat out of those "flavorful little packages," and it is my opinion that you will beg to go out to the yard to pick them up instead!

Another treasure Louisiana can claim is the late African-American artist Clementine Hunter. She didn't begin her artistic pursuit until she was about 50 years old, then she painted for nearly another 50 years, living until she was 101 (1886–1988). Her lifetime body of work includes more than 5,000 objects of art.

Growing up on Melrose Plantation in Natchitoches, Louisiana, Hunter worked first in the fields, then she was "promoted" to housework and cooking in the main house. A self-taught artist, she used almost any flat surface to apply her paints. Some of her work appears on old window shades, cardboard boxes, bottles and pieces of fabric.

Known for representing daily life as she saw it firsthand, Hunter painted scenes of picking cotton, washing clothes, getting married and getting buried. Fortunately for us, she painted a charming picture entitled *Threshing Pecans* (below), portraying an earlier, preindustrial method of coaxing the nuts from the trees to the ground—adults would use long poles to shake the pecans while children climbed up into the trees to help in the process.

Although she was born into obscurity, Clementine Hunter lived all her life in and around Natchitoches and died a celebrated artist. Her work is included in numerous private collections and can be seen in some museums on permanent exhibit. In recent years, some of her paintings have been reproduced on high-quality dishware manufactured in Portugal and sold at Melrose Plantation (see page 171).

Now iconic, Hunter is sometimes referred to as the "black Grandma Moses" and her name is synonymous with the best in primitive art.

167

Courtesy Tom Whitehead

Threshing Pecans by Clementine Hunter

ACKNOWLEDGMENTS

Writing this book was arduous fun. Pleasure came from immersing myself in the subject of pecans. Pain came from having to decide when to stop praising the nut. There were more recipes and decidedly additional good things to say about pecans, but the end had to come at some point.

A lot of the pleasure came from the fact that doors opened easily, and I received so much encouragement from people who commented,

"I'm so glad you're writing a book about pecans; they're my favorite nut! How can I help?"

Friends, academics, and commercial growers and shellers all contributed greatly to bringing this book to light. Without them, I would have toiled, sometimes in darkness, without the knowledge required to discuss pecans intelligently.

Without them, I would not have been able to visit orchards during harvest and pick up a nut

168

off the ground, crack it and eat it right under the tree. Certainly, without them, I would have missed out on a lot of what my grandmother used to call "good, clean fun!"

Thanks to everyone who is mentioned here, as well as to anyone else who works tirelessly to bring a high-quality nut to the consumer. After all, to know pecans is to love them ... but first, you have to eat a really good one.

- Colleen and Sam Nunn
- Ethelynn and Bill Stuckey
- Pat and Bob Schieffer
- Rue Judd, Publisher, Bright Sky Press
- Kristine Krueger, Editor
- Isabel Lasater Hernandez, Designer
- Watt M. Casey, Jr., Photographer
- Dr. Bill Goff, Extension Horticulturist–Pecans and Professor, Auburn University, Alabama
- Dr. L.J. Grauke, Research Horticulturist for the USDA ARS Pecan Breeding Program and Curator of the National Collection of Genetic Resources for Pecans and Hickories, Texas A&M University
- Dr. Leonardo Lombardini, Assistant Professor, Department of Horticultural Sciences, Texas A&M University
- Dr. Niels Maness, Professor, Department of Horticulture and Landscape Architecture, Oklahoma State University

- Bill McGehee, Pecan Grower, Big Six Farm, Fort Valley, Georgia
- Mary and Al Pearson, Pearson Farm and Big Six Farm, Fort Valley, Georgia
- William S. Morris III, Pecan Grower, Wade Plantation, Sylvania, Georgia
- H.J. Bergeron Company, Pecan Shellers, New Roads, Louisiana
- Eleanor and Tommy Hatfield, owners of Kinloch Plantation Products, Pecan Oil Distributors, Winnsboro, Louisiana
- Tom Whitehead, President, Cane River Art Corporation, friend of Clementine Hunter and a collector of her works

—June Jackson

169

Special thanks to Winston, Kristen and Anna Elizabeth Millican and Winston's parents, Bob and Debbie, of Millican Pecan Company, San Saba, Texas, for opening their lives and pecan business to me in 2006. I appreciate the many contributions that Sam and Colleen Nunn made, for opening their home to me and for being gracious hosts while in St. Simons Island and Sea Island, Georgia. And to my wife, Shelley, who allows me to make these excursions that Rue and Bright Sky Press come up with, *saludos y abrazos con amor.*

—Watt M. Casey, Jr.

SOURCE GUIDE

Now that you've read the book and are ready to try some of the recipes, you might discover the need for reliable sources for high-quality pecans. The following entries are only a partial listing; these are simply tested venues that sell both good pecans and fresh pecan oil.

The Web sites make for good reading as well, as a few of the companies include historical material about their businesses, particularly those based on plantations. Many sell pecan delicacies, gift packs and other items along with raw pecans.

ALABAMA

B&B Pecan Co.
16151 Greeno Rd. (Hwy. 98)
Fairhope AL 36532
800/732-6812
pecangifts.com

Dees Pecan Co.
6328 Grand Bay-Wilmer Rd.
Grand Bay AL 36541
251/865-1040

Priester's Pecans
208 Old Fort Rd. E.
Fort Deposit AL 36032
800/277-3226
priesters.com

Tucker Pecan Co.
350 N. McDonough St.
Montgomery AL 36104
800/239-6540
tuckerpecan.com

ARIZONA

The Farmer's House
711 E. Carefree Hwy. # 224
Phoenix AZ 85085
623/910-9033

The Green Valley Pecan Co.
1625 E. Sahuarita Rd.
Sahuarita AZ 85629
520/791-2852
greenvalleypecan.com

ARKANSAS

York Pecan Co.
2919 Hwy. 32
Foreman AR 71836
866/370-1607
yorkpecan.com

FLORIDA

Renfroe Pecans
2400 W. Fairfield Dr.
Pensacola FL 32505
800/874-1929
renfroepecan.com

GEORGIA

Big Six Farm
5575 Zenith Mill Rd.
Fort Valley GA 31030
478/825-7504
bigsixfarm.com

Ellis Bros. Pecans
1315 Tippettville Rd.
Vienna GA 31092
800/635-0616
werenuts.com

Harrell Nut Co.
275 Industrial Blvd.
Camilla GA 31730
800/526-8770
harrellnut.com

Lane Packing Co.
50 Lane Rd.
Fort Valley GA 31030
800/277-3224
lanepacking.com

Merritt Pecan Co.
Hwy. 520, P.O. Box 39
Weston GA 31832
800/762-9152
merritt-pecan.com

Pearson Farm
11022 Hwy. 341
Fort Valley GA 31030
888/423-7374
pearsonfarm.com

Peyton's Pecan Orchard
5824 Hwy. 97
Camilla GA 31730
866/739-8607
peytonspecans.com

Schermer Pecans
819 S. Downing Musgrove Hwy.
Glennville GA 30427
800/841-3403
pecantreats.com

South Georgia Pecan Co.
309 S. Lee St.
Valdosta GA 31603
800/627-6630
georgiapecan.com

Wade Plantation Pecans
752 Oglethorpe Tr.
Sylvania GA 30167
800/414-7941
wadepecans.com

LOUISIANA
Bayou Country General Store
1101 E. Howze Beach Rd.
Slidell LA 70461
888/571-3200
bayoucountry.com

Cane River Pecan Co.
1415 East St.
New Iberia LA 70560
800/293-8710
caneriverpecans.com

Classic Golden Pecans
4303 Johnston St.
Lafayette LA 70503
(Texas location: 411 W. Main St.,
Tomball 77375)
888/663-2137
classicgoldenpecans.com

Kinloch Plantation Products
1304 Cornell St.
Winnsboro LA 71295
318/435-1455

Melrose Plantation
("Threshing Pecans" dishware
available here; see page 167)
3533 Hwy. 119
Melrose LA 71452
318/379-0055

Natchitoches Pecans
439 Little Eva Rd.
Cloutierville LA 71416
800/572-5925
natchitochespecans.com

Rosalie Pecans
51 Rosalie Rd.
Alexandria LA 71302
877/772-3139
rosaliepecans.com

MISSISSIPPI
Bass Pecan Co.
P.O. Box 2465
Madison MS 39130
800/732-2671
basspecan.net

Indianola Pecan House
1013 Hwy. 82 E.
Indianola MS 38751
800/541-6252
pecanhouse.com

Smith's Pecans
19825 Hwy. 18
Raymond MS 39154
888/857-5987
smithspecans.com

171

MISSOURI
Stark Bros.
(a good outlet for pecan seedlings to plant)
800/325-4180
starkbros.com

NEW MEXICO
Ritch's Pecan & Candy Shoppe
HC 30, Box 8
Cuchillo NM 87901
505/743-3201

Stahmanns Country Store
22505 S. Hwy. 28
San Miguel NM 88058
505/525-3470
stahmanns.com

Tularosa Pecan Co.
121 Bookout Rd. N.E.
Tularosa NM 88352
800/732-2678
tularosapecan.com

OKLAHOMA
Benson Park Pecans
41502 Benson Park Rd.
Shawnee OK 74801
405/273-1235
bensonparkpecans.com

Bryant Pecan Co.
100 E. 9th St.
Ada OK 74820
580/332-0839
enjoypecans.com

Schoenecke Bros. Pecans
Rt. 2, Box 272B
Meeker OK 74855
405/788-5091

Valley Grove Pecans
2301 E. 151st St.
Bixby OK 74008
888/442-9190

OREGON
Patricia's Kitchen
55015 Huntington Rd.
Sunriver OR 97707
541/593-9116

SOUTH CAROLINA
Golden Kernel Pecan Co.
408 Old Orangeburg Rd.
Cameron SC 29030
800/845-2448
goldenkernel.com

Young Pecan Plantations
551 W. Lucas St. *(outlet)*
Florence SC 29501
800/729-6003
youngpecanplantations.com

TEXAS
Ara Pecan Corp.
426 St. James St.
Gonzales TX 78629
800/299-6887
arapecan.com

Berdoll Pecan Farm
2626 Hwy. 71 W.
Cedar Creek TX 78612
800/518-3870
berdoll.com

Boney and Claud's Pecan Emporium
311 N. High (Hwy. 16 N.)
San Saba TX 76877
325/372-6887
boneyandclauds.com

Durham-Ellis Pecans
Three locations: Hwy. 377 E.,
   Comanche 76442, 800/732-2629
   6964 Green Oaks Rd., Fort Worth
   76116, 817/989-2818
   804 Fisher, Goldthwaite 76844,
   325/648-2746
durhampecan.com

Foster Crossing Pecans
1320 CR 366
Anna TX 75409
972/838-2321
fostercrossingpecans.com

LeBlanc's Pecan Co.
2032 Hwy. 90A
Richmond TX 77469
800/890-1188
leblancspecancompany.com

McCain's Market
550 Heights Blvd. Suite C
Houston TX 77008
713/869-0011
mccainsmarket.com

Millican Pecan Co.
1101 W. Wallace
San Saba TX 76877
866/484-6358
pecancompany.com

Oliver Pecan Co.
1402 W. Wallace
San Saba TX 76877
800/657-9291
oliverpecan.com

Pape Pecan House
101 S. Hwy. 123 Bypass
Seguin TX 78155
830/379-7442
papepecan.com

Pecans.com
1700 N. Bryant Blvd.
San Angelo TX 76903
800/437-2267
pecans.com

Pecans International
5148 E. Hwy. 158
Gardendale TX 79758
888/367-3226
pecansinternational.com

Pecan Shed
1401 Midwestern Pkwy.
Wichita Falls TX 76302
800/317-3226
pecanshed.com

Potter Country Store
10926 Hwy. 77
Schulenburg TX 78956
877/743-2660
pottercountrystore.com

Ramirez Pecan Farm
13709 N. Loop Dr.
Clint TX 79836
915/851-2003
ramirezpecanfarm.com

Southern Select Nut Co.
1113 N. Fulton
Wharton TX 77488
979/531-8080
southernselectnut.com

Tobias Pecans
109 E. State Hwy. 71
Ellinger TX 78938
979/378-2829
tobiaspecans.com

Valley Pecans
1001 Hwy. 287
Chillicothe TX 79225
940/852-5957
valleypecans.com

Weatherford Central Market
3115 Fort Worth Hwy. Suite 100
Weatherford TX 76087
817/599-5819
4thebestpecans.com

173

RECIPE INDEX

174

175